THE BEST OF SOUTHERN ITALIAN COOKING

J.C. GRASSO

FOR MY MOTHER AND
IN MEMORY OF MY FATHER

First paperback edition 1994.

© Copyright 1984 by Jean Grasso Fitzpatrick.

All inquiries should be addressed to:
Barron's Educational Series, Inc.
250 Wireless Boulevard
Hauppauge, New York 11788

Photographic Credits

Color photographs: Matthew Klein
Food styling: Andrea Swenson
Photo styling: Linda Cheverton
Props used are courtesy of the following: sterling silver from
  Buccellati, Inc., New York; crystal from Baccarat, New
  York; antique oak table from Pierre Deux Antiques, New
  York; flowers by Ann Titus, New York; antique Sicilian
  puppet from Geppetto's Toys, Inc., New York.

Book design   Milton Glaser, Inc.

International Standard Book No. 0-8120-1990-3
Library of Congress Catalog Card No. 84-11048

Library of Congress Cataloging in Publication Data
Grasso, J. C. (Jean C.)
   The best of southern Italian cooking.

   Includes index.
   1. Cookery, Italian.   I. Title
TX723.G755   1984   641.5945'7   84-11048
ISBN 0-8120-1990-3 (pbk)
ISBN 0-8120-5483-0

PRINTED IN HONG KONG BY WING KING TONG CO., LTD.

5 6 7   790   9 8 7 6 5 4 3 2

Contents

Preface

This is a cookbook with a mission. Its aim is to persuade you, the food lover and cook, that the cuisines of southern Italy are every bit as fascinating and varied as their currently fashionable northern counterparts, and that the culinary traditions of the Italian South make perfect sense as part of the contemporary American diet. If you believe that southern Italian cooking means tomatoes, tomatoes, and more tomatoes simmered for hours into overspiced, heavy sauces, I hope the recipes on the following pages will change your mind.

Exploring an ancient cuisine is always fascinating because every traditional dish reflects centuries of history—conquests, climate, and economy—and southern Italy's is no exception. Although I have included recipes that survive from the kitchens of the nobility, southern Italian cooking is most of all a triumph of *la cucina povera,* the cuisine of the poor people who worked feudal lands and had neither the time nor the means to prepare twelve-course extravaganzas. But they learned to work wonders with the fruits and vegetables and fish of the world around them. Many of the recipes in this book are ideal for the vegetarian dining that has now become popular all across the United States, because southern Italian cooks, whose supply of meat has always been scarce, can make magic with vegetables and grains. For the most part, these recipes are easy to prepare. I have included a number of showstoppers that are perfect for dinner parties, but most of the dishes are gloriously simple, designed to make everyday eating an exciting and healthy exploration of the tastes of southern Italy.

Acknowledgments

For their enthusiasm and assistance, I would like to thank Stephen
S. Hall; Joan Field Esposito; Richard Ticktin; Maria and Enzo
Serpotta; Adolfo de Martino of the Jolly Hotels; Paolo Seminara;
Giovanna Cangialosi of the Ente Provinciale di Turismo in Palermo, whose research and inside tips proved invaluable; and Emilia
Medwied of the Italian Government Travel Office in New York,
who devoted a great deal of time and energy to facilitating my
research in Italy. I also owe a debt of gratitude to the many friends
who sampled the recipes; to my aunt and uncle Eda and Carmen
Grasso; my brother, Louis; my mother; and my husband Des Fitzpatrick, who learned to communicate in Italian, went grocery
shopping, and washed many pots and pans; without his loving
encouragement I could not have written this book.

Introduction

The sun shines brightly on the dramatic landscapes of southern Italy, and that is why Italians call the area the Mezzogiorno—high noon, the brightest time of day. Many American travelers have gazed on the breathtaking vistas of the South—the hills topped with fig and olive trees all over Sicily, the fishing villages that dot the Amalfi coast like jewels, the cliffs edged in bougainvillea that drop away to the bay at Capri. Yet few visitors—and fewer still of those who never make the trip—ever sample the regions' authentic tastes; Sicily's exotic sweet-and-sour pasta, Bari's fragrant potato tielle, and the shellfish creations of Naples are hardly known on our shores. It's puzzling that the South, which sent so many of its sons and daughters to the United States at the height of Italian migration, kept its glorious culinary secrets at home.

Sadly, now that Americans have at last come to appreciate the subtleties of Italian food and no longer associate it with oily, oversauced pizza-parlor fare, northern cuisine has stolen the show. In fact, a new myth has been born. Now many Americans believe that the spaghetti and meatballs and the sausage and peppers they ate as children were southern Italian foods. You'll learn otherwise if you ask a southern Italian—or an American whose family hailed from Caserta, Catania, or Bari—about the food he or she remembers from childhood. You're likely to hear of marvelous tastes and smells from the kitchen of *nonna* (grandmother): soups fragrant with herbs, couscous steamed in fish broth, elaborate pastries bursting with almonds, ricotta, and generous handfuls of imagination.

Americans aren't the only ones who have neglected the Mezzogiorno's traditional gastronomic delights. For quite a while, even the natives were content to let them lapse into memory. Several Sicilian chefs have told me that for years none of their compatriots would touch fava beans, for example, because they were associated with centuries of dire poverty—they were "poor people's food." It is only recently that the ingenuity of *la cucina povera* has come to be appreciated by today's more affluent Italians, and dishes such as Maccu, the ancient soup of pureed fava beans flavored with olive oil and wild fennel, have reappeared on Sicilian tables—and even today they are not served frequently.

For that reason, until the past few years, tourists in southern Italy were unlikely to enjoy authentic local specialties, unless they ventured down one of the *vicoli* (alleyways) of old Naples for a pizza baked in a wood-fired oven, or had the good fortune to be offered a home-cooked meal. I once arrived in a small Calabrian town and asked a native if there were any restaurants where I could sample local specialties. He looked puzzled. "People here can eat those at home," he said. "Why would they pay to eat them in a restaurant?" Fortunately, that philosophy no longer prevails, and today many restaurants proudly feature regional dishes. Their owners and chefs, as well as many home cooks, were eager to share recipes for this book.

The Southern Regions

Southern Italy and Sicily encompass five political divisions, or regions, south of Rome. *Campania,* the breathtakingly beautiful area whose capital is Naples, is famed both for its glorious sunshine and lovely panoramic views, from the bay of Naples to the dramatic Amalfi Drive, and its tragic history of natural disasters, from the Vesuvian eruption that buried Pompeii to the 1980 earthquake that leveled mountain villages and sections of Naples. *Apulia,* the eastern region that runs along the heel of the Italian boot, has the longest coastline of any Italian region and boasts two gracious cities, traditional centers of trade with the east, Bari and Brindisi. *Calabria*—Italy's toe—was an important part of Magna Graecia, as was Apulia. Mountainous and a significant producer of citrus fruits, Calabria is the second poorest region in Italy, despite a glorious history. The pleasure lovers of Sybaris, its chief city under the Greeks, gave us our word for one who loves pampering and luxury; Sybarites were said to have crowned their most creative cook. *Basilicata,* known in ancient times and during the Fascist period as Lucania, lies south of Campania and north of Calabria on the Mediterranean. It is stark, remote, and mountainous, the smallest and poorest region in Italy. *Sicily,* the largest island in the Mediterranean, is also mountainous. Most of its population is clustered along its three coasts—the Tyrrhenian (north), Mediterranean (South) and Ionian (east)—but it grows vegetables and citrus fruits for much of Europe.

Southern Italian cooking, like its northern counterpart, varies from region to region, province to province, and even village to village, reflecting diversity in geography, climate, and history. The Sicilian table, for example, bears the stamp of the island's tumultuous centuries of conquest; each dish reflects the influence of one or more invaders—especially the Greeks, Arabs, and Spanish. The Campanian flair for cooking with vegetables came naturally, thanks to the abundance and flavor of the produce grown in the fertile volcanic soil around Mount Vesuvius; a centuries-long reign of Naples as one of Europe's premier cities left a legacy of countless tomato dishes, after the fruit was brought back from the New World by the city's Spanish rulers. Apulians enjoy the tender fish of the Adriatic and produce countless grain-based dishes from the fruit of their fertile plains. Calabria and Basilicata, triumphing over scarcity, make use of every bit of pork to be had to produce their famous sausages and hams.

Yet a number of characteristics are common to all of the regions of southern Italy, and it is these characteristics that make traditional southern Italian cooking perfectly suited to the contemporary style of American dining. First of all, the cuisine is based on simple combinations of ingredients; the cream- and butter-based sauces that enrich many popular northern dishes are virtually unheard of in the Mezzogiorno. Olive oil is used, but not with a heavy hand (as it is in pizza-parlor cooking), because in poverty-stricken southern Italy, the fruit of the olive was almost as precious as gold. Second, Americans are now eating less meat, and southern Italian cooking offers a refreshing change of pace for the vegetarian who is not always in the mood for tofu or wheat germ. Since cows had to be used as beasts of burden and chickens were kept alive to lay eggs, the cooks of this area learned to be inventive without using meat.

Needless to say, *la cucina povera* requires no frantic, wallet-emptying shopping expeditions in search of luxury items such as white truffles, dried wild mushrooms, or extravirgin olive oil. The intelligent use of fresh—fresh!—local ingredients is the hallmark of southern Italian cooking. Beef, whole fish, and fine cheeses were beyond the means of most southern Italians, but they could work miracles with ground meat, "trash" fish, simple melted cheeses, and flavorful vegetables. If you follow their example and insist on the freshest ingredients, you, too, will be able to work magic on a low grocery budget.

A prevailing misconception about Italian cooking is that it requires that the cook spend hours stirring sauces at a hot stove. Nothing could be further from the truth. Dishes like pasta with sautéed vegetables can be made in the time it takes the noodles to cook. And even spectacular dishes like Ripiddu Nivicatu, the miniature Mount Etna made of rice and calamari with ricotta, are invariably a matter of assembly rather than painstaking technique. The people of the Mezzogiorno worked hard, usually for absentee feudal lords, and they had little time for virtuoso performances except on feast days.

Happily, in many southern Italian kitchens hardship inspired not only inventiveness but a sense of humor as well. Sicily's Lasagne Cacate (shitty noodles) were originally so called to poke fun at the elegantly named dishes of the nobility. At times the whimsy was irreverent: the Sicilian Minni di Virgini cookies, for example, are soft meringues shaped into ''breasts of the Virgin.''

Sicily's Contribution

Of all the cuisines of the South, Sicily's is without a doubt the one that most brilliantly reflects the area's fascinating past, and virtually every Sicilian recipe is an edible history lesson. Sicily attracted Greek pirates as early as the fifth century B.C., and once the Greeks settled in, they planted olive trees and vineyards, building a considerable reputation for Sicilian wines. As early as the fourth century B.C. Archestratus of Syracuse wrote a mock epic on the pleasures of gastronomy, in which he waxed poetic on the Sicilian cooking of the day. Tuna with salt, oil, and spices, he said, was ''a food excellent enough to make the gods salivate.'' The Romans planted wheat in Sicily, turning the island into the empire's granary. Pliny the Elder wrote that Ceres taught milling and breadmaking in Sicily, and that is why she was considered a goddess.

Following various other invaders, including the Byzantines, the Arabs, who had started attacking Sicily as early as the seventh century, took Palermo by A.D. 831 and plundered Syracuse by 878. This conquest proved to be a blessing in disguise: Sicily's economy prospered as irrigation improved, rice was planted, citrus groves spread over the hills of Catania and Palermo, and date palms, sugar cane, saffron, cinnamon, cloves, sesame, and other exotica brought new tastes into the island's kitchens. The Arabs started the tuna hunts, introduced couscous and marzapane (marzipan), and may have brought coffee to Sicily at this time. Arabic became the official language, and today many famous Sicilian dishes have Arabic names: the ricotta cake Cassata takes its name from the *quas'at*, a big round pan in which it was made, and Cubbaita, the torrone made with honey, sesame seeds, and almonds, comes from the Arabic *qubbayt*. The Arab geographer

Idrisi noted that vermicelli were being made here as early as A.D. 1154—a century before the birth of Marco Polo—and many Sicilians claim that pasta originated on their island—though Neapolitans beg to differ. Although many traditional Sicilian dishes are termed Arab legacies, they are more accurately said to have been born in Sicily as the offspring of the Sicilian and Arab traditions. The Pasticcio di Pollo of the Emir of Catania is a good example, since it contains olives, capers, and other ingredients introduced prior to the Arab conquest but reflects the Arabic penchant for stuffed foods as well as the use of pistachio nuts. The Arabs also influenced meal structure. Although most Italians insist on a first course of pasta or rice followed by a meat or fish dish, under the Arabs, Sicilians acquired a repertory of one-dish meals such as Riso al Forno. Several Sicilian food writers make a case for the invention of risotto alla milanese in Sicily. After all, they point out, the Arabs did have rice, saffron, onions, and broth, and rice arrived in Lombardy later on by way of the Aragonese of Sicily.

The Normans conquered Sicily during the eleventh century, fusing the Western and Arabic civilizations, and fashionable Normans were seen parading the streets of Palermo in desert robes. But by the twelfth century, after Frederick Barbarossa married off his son Henry to a Sicilian heiress, their son, Frederick II, was crowned Holy Roman Emperor, and Sicily became a part of the empire. Frederick's court was a bastion of high culture (the *scuola siciliana* of poetry greatly influenced Dante), and this was a time when class distinctions became entrenched. Even today two separate traditions of high and low cuisine persist. During the thirteenth century, Sicily and Naples were joined by arrangement of the pope under the French house of Anjou, and high cuisine took on some decidedly Gallic touches. The Sicilian Farsumagru, for example, was first called *rollò*, derived from the French *roulé*. That arrangement ended with the Sicilian Vespers: Sicilians killed off their French invaders, recognizing them by their inability to pronounce the word *cíciri* (toasted chickpeas) properly.

The Spanish ruled southern Italy from the fifteenth to the seventeenth centuries, and it was then that the tomato made its appearance in the kitchens of the Mezzogiorno. By 1718, the Austrian Hapsburgs had taken over Sicily, but the French returned a century later and stayed until 1860, when Garibaldi and his Red Shirts landed at Marsala—where, legend has it, he sipped the city's famous fortified wine—and conquered the island in less than three months.

The recipes in this book offer you the opportunity to share in southern Italy and Sicily's rediscovery of an exciting culinary heritage. If you have dismissed southern Italian cooking as monotonous, heavy, and drowning in tomatoes, the diversity among the recipes in the pages that follow is bound to be a source of continuing and delectable surprise.

Antipasti, Fritti, & Uova

Antipasti, Fritti, & Uova

ANTIPASTI, FRIED THINGS, AND EGGS

It's hard to imagine how the offerings at southern Italian tavole calde and restaurant antipasti displays could be more savory or colorful, and as a result I had a hard time understanding why Sicilians maintain that there is no such thing as a traditional Sicilian antipasto. After considerable investigation, I learned that what they mean is that the dishes we think of today as appetizers once served as breakfast, lunch, and dinner in the Sicilian peasant households. In other words, that's all the family had to eat. That undoubtedly accounts for the extraordinary imaginativeness that characterizes every dish.

Practically anything can be made into a fritter or croquette—artichokes, eggplant, broccoli, and, yes, potatoes. But if you think of potato croquettes as humdrum, Sicily's finger-shaped Cazzilli (''little penises'') are bound to change your mind. The southern culinary sense of humor is evident in the names of many of the dishes in this chapter, including Arancine (''little oranges''), which are actually rice balls coated with bread crumbs and fried till they are the color of the citrus fruit, and the Neapolitan Uova 'mpriatorio (''eggs in Purgatory''), eggs poached in a spicy tomato sauce. Many of these recipes can serve, alone, as a light lunch, and several together make a wonderful and colorful antipasto display.

Frittelle di Carciofi

ARTICHOKE FRITTERS

When dropped into hot oil, the spoonfuls of artichoke leaves brushed with batter magically turn into lovely golden fritters that resemble flowers—or, some say, fried chicken. They're suitable as an antipasto, as a side dish, or as part of a frittura mista. Serves 4.

Ingredients

2 large eggs
¼ teaspoon salt
2 cups unbleached all-purpose flour
6 artichokes
Juice of 1 lemon
Olive or sunflower oil for deep-frying

Beat the eggs with the salt, and gradually stir in the flour to form a smooth paste. Add ¼ cup water and continue stirring until the dough is soft and smooth. Set the batter aside to rest for 1 hour.

Trim off the tough outer leaves of the artichokes, cut off the woody ends of the stems, and scrape out the chokes with a small, sharp knife. In a large saucepan of water, simmer the artichokes with the lemon juice until they are tender, about 20 minutes.

Drain the artichokes and pat them dry with paper towels. Cut them into eighths lengthwise. Stir the artichokes into the batter. It will not coat the artichoke leaves and will be hard to handle.

Pour oil into a deep saucepan to a depth of about 4 inches. When it is very hot, deep-fry the artichokes a few at a time. When the fritters are golden and crisp, remove them with a slotted spoon and drain them on paper towels. Serve the frittelle hot.

Antipasto platter with Artichoke Fritters ▶

Polpettine di Broccoli

BREADED BROCCOLI BALLS

Since the vegetable is cooked only until barely tender before being encased in bread crumbs and deep-fried, these croquettes are bursting with the flavor of fresh broccoli. Serves 4

Ingredients

1 seedless hard roll
2 pounds fresh broccoli, stems trimmed
Pinch of salt
1 large egg
2 tablespoons grated parmesan cheese
Black pepper
1 cup bread crumbs for dredging
Olive or sunflower oil for deep-frying

Cover the hard roll with milk and let it soak for about 1 hour. Place the broccoli in a large pot of cold water, bring it to a boil, and add the salt. Cook the broccoli just until it is tender, 8 to 10 minutes. Drain it well and chop it until it is very fine.

Squeeze the milk out of the softened roll and put the roll in a large bowl with the broccoli, egg, Parmesan cheese, and black pepper to taste. Mix well. Mold the mixture with your fingers into small balls, each about 2½ inches in diameter, and roll them in the bread crumbs to coat well.

Pour oil into a small saucepan until it is about ¾ full. When the oil is very hot, deep-fry the broccoli balls two or three at a time until they are golden brown. Drain them on paper towels and serve them hot.

◀ *Fried Mozzarella ''Sandwiches'' (recipe on page 9).*

Frittelle di Melanzane

EGGPLANT BALLS

Don't expect these to taste like eggplant. Actually, they are surprisingly similar in texture to meatballs, even though they are strictly vegetarian. They can serve as a main course or as an antipasto. Serves 4

Ingredients

1 pound eggplant
¾ cup grated pecorino cheese
1 cup bread crumbs
1 clove garlic, minced
1 tablespoon minced fresh Italian parsley
Pinch of freshly grated nutmeg
2 eggs
Flour for dredging
Olive or sunflower oil for deep-frying
1 recipe Tomato Sauce (page 41)

Peel the eggplants and halve them lengthwise. In a large pot of water simmer them for 40 minutes or until they are tender. Mash them in a food mill or processor.

In a mixing bowl combine the mashed eggplant with the cheese, bread crumbs, garlic, parsley, nutmeg, and eggs. Mix well with a wooden spoon. Flour your hands and mold the mixture into little balls. Roll the eggplant balls in the flour.

Pour oil into a small saucepan to a depth of about 2 inches. When it is very hot, deep-fry the eggplant balls two or three at a time until they are crisp and golden. Spoon the Tomato Sauce over them.

Caponata di Melanzane

EGGPLANT CAPONATA

Like many classic Sicilian dishes, this recipe has both humble and aristocratic variations; some call for the addition of shellfish, for example. This one, garnished with toasted nuts and hard-cooked egg, contains a "mystery ingredient"—unsweetened cocoa—which adds an intriguing, bitter note. Despite the long list of ingredients, it's quite simple to make. Serves 4

Ingredients

2 medium eggplants
2 tablespoons slivered almonds
¼ cup olive oil
1 onion, thinly sliced
1 pound tomatoes, peeled, seeded, and chopped
2 stalks celery, chopped
1 green pepper, chopped
⅔ cup green olives, pitted
⅔ cup capers
Salt
3 tablespoons sugar
½ cup wine vinegar
¾ teaspoon unsweetened cocoa
1 hard-cooked egg, sliced (optional)

Cut the eggplants into large chunks and let them soak in salted water for 30 minutes. Drain, rinse well, drain again, and pat dry with paper towels. Set aside.

Preheat the oven to 300° F. and toast the almonds for 10 minutes.

In a skillet, sauté the eggplant chunks in the olive oil and drain them on paper towels. Add the onion, tomatoes, celery, and green pepper to the skillet. Cook the vegetables briefly, stirring constantly, until the onion is soft. Add the olives, capers, the salt to taste, and the sautéed eggplant chunks.

Dissolve the sugar in the vinegar and add it to the pan. Stir in the cocoa and cook the mixture for 10 minutes over low heat. Turn the heat up toward the end to reduce the liquid. Serve the caponata at room temperature garnished with sliced egg, if desired, and toasted almonds.

Frittedda

SICILIAN SWEET-AND-SOUR VEGETABLES

There are many versions of this fried vegetable dish, which traditionally features artichokes. Serves 4

Ingredients

2 pounds dried fava beans
4 artichokes
Juice of 1 lemon
1 small onion, chopped
½ cup olive oil
Pinch of freshly grated nutmeg
Salt and black pepper
1½ pounds fresh peas, shelled
2 tablespoons sugar
4 tablespoons wine vinegar

Soak the fava beans overnight in water to cover. Cook them in a large pot of water for 1 hour or until they are tender. (Or you can use frozen fava beans cooked according to the package directions.)

Trim the stems off the artichokes and remove the tough outer leaves. Cut the artichokes in half and remove the chokes with a small, sharp knife. Cut the artichokes into eighths lengthwise and cook them in a saucepan of water with the lemon juice until they are tender, about 20 minutes.

In a large skillet sauté the onion in the oil until it is transparent. Add the artichokes and sauté them until they are light golden. Sprinkle them with the nutmeg and salt and pepper to taste.

Reduce the heat to low and add the fava beans and peas to the skillet. Cover and cook until the peas are tender, about 10 minutes, adding 3 or 4 tablespoons of water if necessary to keep the frittedda from sticking to the pan.

Dissolve the sugar in the vinegar and sprinkle the liquid over the vegetables. Toss the mixture well and turn it out onto a serving plate. Let frittedda cool before serving.

Mozzarella in Carozza

FRIED MOZZARELLA "SANDWICHES"

Fresh snow-white mozzarella, not the rubbery packaged kind, is essential for this Neapolitan classic. Serves 4. Photo opposite page 5.

Ingredients

1 loaf Italian bread
½ pound fresh mozzarella
2 large eggs
½ cup milk
Flour for dredging
Sunflower oil for deep-frying

Remove the crust from the bread and cut the loaf into eight slices; then cut each slice in half. Cut the cheese into eight slices. Make eight small "sandwiches" by placing each slice of cheese between two half-slices of bread.

Beat the eggs and milk together with a fork until they are well mixed. Dredge the sandwiches in flour and then dip them in the egg-milk mixture.

Pour oil into a small saucepan to a depth of about 3 inches. When it is very hot, lower the sandwiches into it carefully, one at a time, and deep-fry them until they are golden brown and puffy. Drain them on paper towels and serve them immediately.

Arancine

STUFFED RICE BALLS

Citrus fruits are almost synonymous with Sicily, and so are arancine, ''little oranges.'' The bread-crumb coating on these balls of rice stuffed with peas and ground beef turns a deep gold during the frying, making them resemble real oranges—another example of the Sicilian penchant for playful names. They are a ubiquitous snack food. Serves 4. Photo 1 opposite page 20.

Ingredients

Pinch of saffron
3 cups rice
1 teaspoon salt
1 onion, finely chopped
2 tablespoons olive oil
½ pound lean ground beef
1 cup fresh or frozen green peas, cooked
¼ cup dry white wine
1 teaspoon dried rosemary
3 large eggs, separated
1¾ cups grated caciocavallo or pecorino cheese
Flour for dredging
¾ cup bread crumbs
Sunflower oil for deep-frying

Dissolve the saffron in ½ cup warm water. Place the rice in a saucepan with the saffron water and add 5½ cups of water. Add the salt and bring the water to a boil. Immediately lower the heat, cover, and simmer until the water is absorbed and the rice is tender, about 20 minutes. Let the rice cool to room temperature.

In a large skillet, sauté the onion in the oil until it is transparent. Add the ground meat and cook the mixture, stirring, until it loses its raw red color. Add the peas and the wine and cook until the wine evaporates. Season with rosemary and salt to taste. Add the egg yolks and grated cheese to the cooked rice and mix well.

Beat the egg whites briefly with a fork. Brush about ½ teaspoon of egg white on the palm of your hand, press 2 heaping tablespoons of rice into it, and mold it into a hollow, cuplike shell. Fill the hollow with 1 tablespoon of the meat mixture. Cover the filling with 1 tablespoon of rice and use both hands to seal the filling inside and shape the stuffed rice into a ball about the size of a small orange. Roll each arancina first in flour, then in the remaining egg white, and finally in the bread crumbs.

Pour oil into a small saucepan to a depth of about 4 inches. When it is very hot, deep-fry the arancine two or three at a time, turning occasionally, until they are golden brown on all sides. Drain them on paper towels and serve them warm.

Arancine al Burro

RICE BALLS FILLED WITH BUTTER AND CHEESE

This is a meatless version of Sicily's popular arancine. The saffron-colored rice encases a nugget of melted cheese, butter, and peas. These arancine are ordinarily made with primu sale, the very young sheep's-milk cheese found only in Sicily, but fresh white mozzarella, *at room temperature so that it will melt*, is a good substitute. Serves 6

Ingredients

1½ cups rice
½ cup grated pecorino cheese
1 large egg, lightly beaten
Pinch of saffron
½ pound (2 sticks) butter, softened
½ pound fresh mozzarella cheese
¼ cup fresh or frozen peas, cooked
2 large eggs, beaten
¾ cup bread crumbs
Sunflower oil for deep-frying

Place the rice in a saucepan with 3 cups of water and bring it to a boil. Lower the heat to a gentle simmer, cover, and cook for 20 minutes until the water is absorbed and the rice is tender. Stir in the grated pecorino cheese, the lightly beaten egg, and the saffron water. Let the mixture cool to room temperature.

Press 2 heaping tablespoons of rice into the palm of your hand and mold it into a hollow, cuplike shell. Fill the hollow with 1 tablespoon of butter, 1 tablespoon of mozzarella cheese, and four or five peas. Cover the filling with 1 tablespoon of rice and use both hands to seal the filling inside and shape the stuffed rice into a ball. Do not make these arancine too big. If you do, the mozzarella cheese inside them will not melt. Aim for the size of tangerines and be sure that the mozzarella cheese is at room temperature when you begin.

Roll each arancina first in the flour, then in the beaten egg, and finally in the bread crumbs.

Pour olive oil into a small saucepan to a depth of about 4 inches. When it is very hot, deep-fry the rice balls two or three at a time, turning them occasionally, until they are golden brown on all sides. Drain them on paper towels and serve them hot.

Cazzilli

POTATO CROQUETTES

If you've always considered potato croquettes boring fare for bridge nights and school cafeterias, the Sicilian perspective is bound to come as a surprise. Sicilians aren't at all bashful about the fact that the word *cazzilli* is the plural diminutive for the male sex organ; you can order these potato-cheese snacks in virtually any tavola calda on the island. Serves 10

Ingredients

2 pounds potatoes
2 large eggs, separated
¼ cup freshly grated pecorino cheese
¾ cup and 3 tablespoons bread crumbs
1 clove garlic
1 tablespoon fresh Italian parsley
Salt and black pepper
Olive oil for deep-frying

Peel and quarter the potatoes. Cook them, covered, in lightly salted water for 20 minutes or until they are tender. Cool the potatoes and put them through a sieve or ricer. Mix the egg yolks with the riced potatoes and add the grated cheese and the 3 tablespoons of bread crumbs.

Chop the garlic together with the parsley to make a homogenous mince. Add it to the potato mixture, along with salt and pepper to taste. Mold a heaping tablespoonful of the potato mixture into a cylinder about the size of your thumb. Repeat the procedure with the remaining mixture to form the cazzilli.

In a small bowl, beat the egg whites lightly with a fork. Dip the cazzilli in the egg whites and then roll them in the ¾ cup bread crumbs. Pour olive oil into a small saucepan to a depth of about 2 inches. When it is very hot, deep-fry the cazzilli two or three at a time until they are golden. Drain them on paper towels and serve them hot or lukewarm.

La Pizza

PIZZA DOUGH

The classic treat of Naples has acquired undeserved notoriety in this country on two counts: people think it's too much trouble to make, and they consider it junk food. Actually, you can make the crust in surprisingly little time, especially if you have a food processor, and some of the simplest toppings are the best. As for nutritional value, pizza is almost a perfect food as long as you make it with real cheese and a minimum of olive oil. Use this dough to make pizza and the Ripieno al Forno (page 20), kneading by hand or in a food processor. Serves 4

Ingredients

1 package active dry yeast
¼ teaspoon sugar
2½ cups unbleached all-purpose flour
1 teaspoon salt
¼ cup olive oil

By Hand

In a small bowl dissolve the yeast and the sugar in ¼ cup warm water (115° F.). Let the mixture stand for 10 minutes or until foam forms on top.

In a large bowl, combine 1 cup of the flour with the salt and add yeast mixture. Stir in the olive oil and add the rest of the flour gradually, mixing with a wooden spoon. Keep working in the flour by hand, kneading until the dough is smooth, elastic, and no longer sticky. The amount of flour you need to use will depend on the weather and on the amount of moisture in the flour you're using.

Turn the dough out into an oiled bowl, turning it to coat all sides. Turn on the oven at the lowest setting, leave it on for 2 minutes, and then turn it off. Set the bowl of dough in the oven, using a potholder as a cushion, and cover it with a damp towel. Close the oven door and let the dough rise in the oven for 1 hour or until it has doubled in size. Test the dough by pressing two fingers into it; if your fingers leave an imprint, the dough has doubled in size.

In a Food Processor

In a small bowl dissolve the yeast and the sugar in ¼ cup warm water (115° F.). Let the mixture stand for 10 minutes or until foam forms on the top. With the metal blade or dough blade in place, put the yeast mixture, 1 cup of flour, and the salt into the work bowl of the processor. Process for a few seconds, just long enough to mix.

With the machine running, pour the olive oil into the work bowl through the feed tube. Add the rest of the flour ½ cup at a time, processing for 45 seconds after each addition until the mixture forms a ball and is smooth, elastic, and no longer sticky. The amount of flour you need to use will depend on the weather and on the amount of moisture in the flour you're using.

Turn the dough out into an oiled bowl, turning it to coat all sides. Turn on the oven at the lowest setting, leave it on for 2 minutes, and then turn it off. Set the bowl of dough in the oven, using a potholder as a cushion, and cover it with a damp towel. Let the dough rise in the oven with the door closed for 1 hour or until it has doubled in size. Test the dough by pressing two fingers into it; if your fingers leave an imprint, the dough has doubled in size.

Pizza Margherita

PIZZA WITH TOMATOES AND MOZZARELLA

This is the simplest Neapolitan pizza, named for a queen of Italy who liked it. Americans commonly refer to it as "plain" pizza, but there's nothing plain at all about the combination of garden-fresh plum tomatoes, fruity olive oil, snow-white mozzarella cheese, and fragrant fresh basil. For a crust that's as close to authentic as you can get without a wood-fired oven, line your oven rack with a pizza stone manufactured for the purpose (available in specialty cookware shops), or several quarry tiles from a home-improvement store. Serves 2

Ingredients

1 recipe Pizza Dough (page 14)
Cornmeal
1¾ cups fresh plum tomatoes, peeled, seeded, and chopped
¾ pound fresh mozzarella cheese, thinly sliced
½ cup chopped fresh basil
2 tablespoons grated Parmesan cheese
2 tablespoons olive oil

Preheat the oven to 500° F. and heat the pizza stone or quarry tiles in the oven for 30 minutes.

Divide the pizza dough in half and roll it out into 2 rounds, each about 7 inches in diameter. Sprinkle cornmeal on a baking sheet or on a wide wooden spatula called a pizza peel. Place the rounds of dough on the cornmeal. Spread the chopped tomatoes over the pizza dough rounds. Top with the sliced mozzarella cheese and half of the basil. Sprinkle the pies with grated Parmesan cheese and olive oil.

Slip the pies off the peel or the baking sheet directly onto the preheated quarry tiles or pizza stone. If you are not using tiles or a stone, place the baking sheet on the middle rack of the oven. Bake at 500° F. for 15 minutes or until the crusts are golden brown. Sprinkle with the remaining basil and serve each individual pizza on its own plate—just the way it's done in Naples.

Pizza alle Quattro Stagioni

FOUR SEASONS PIZZA

This highly decorative pizza is so named because each quarter has a different topping, making it the original "combination pizza." Vary it by substituting your own favorite toppings. The toppings are separated by strips of dough placed across the pizza like the spokes of a wheel. Using a pizza stone or quarry tiles will produce a better crust, but this pizza is too heavily loaded down with toppings to be transferred directly to the stone. Just place it in the preheated pizza pan right on top of the stone. Serves 2. Photo 2 following page 20.

Ingredients

1 recipe Pizza Dough (page 14)
Cornmeal
1/4 pound prosciutto, thinly sliced
2 tablespoons grated Parmesan cheese
3/4 cup peeled and chopped tomatoes
1/4 pound mozzarella cheese, thinly sliced
3 mussels or littleneck clams, chopped
1 cup thinly sliced mushrooms
1 clove garlic, minced
3 tablespoons olive oil
1 tablespoon fresh or 1 teaspoon dried basil,
chopped or crumbled

Preheat the oven to 500° F. and heat the pizza stone or quarry tiles in the oven for 30 minutes.

Reserve one quarter of the dough and roll out the rest into a circle. Place it on a 15-inch pizza pan or baking sheet sprinkled with cornmeal. Divide the reserved dough into two balls, and roll each ball out into a cylinder equal in length to the diameter of the pizza. Place the cylinders across the pizza at right angles to each other so that they divide the pie into quarters.

Top one quarter with the prosciutto and grated Parmesan cheese; another with half the tomatoes and all of the mozzarella; the third with the mussels or clams; and the fourth with the mushrooms and the remaining tomatoes.

Sprinkle the garlic, olive oil, and basil over the pizza. Bake the pie for 15 minutes at 500° F. or until the crust is golden brown.

Pizza Margherita Bianca

WHITE PIZZA

Pizza without tomatoes is a nice change of pace. Its flavor depends almost entirely on fresh mozzarella and basil. Serves 2

Ingredients

1 recipe Pizza Dough (page 14)
Cornmeal
3/4 pound fresh mozzarella cheese, thinly sliced
1/4 cup chopped fresh basil
3 tablespoons grated Parmesan cheese
2 tablespoons olive oil
salt and freshly ground black pepper to taste

Preheat the oven to 500° F. and heat a pizza stone or quarry tiles in the oven for 30 minutes.

Divide the pizza dough in half and roll it out into 2 rounds, each about 7 inches in diameter. Sprinkle cornmeal on a baking sheet or on a wide spatula called a pizza peel. Place the rounds of dough on the cornmeal. Spread the sliced mozzarella cheese and half of the basil over the pizza dough rounds. Sprinkle the pies with grated Parmesan cheese and olive oil and season to taste with salt and pepper.

Slip the pies off the peel or the baking sheet directly onto the preheated quarry tiles or pizza stone. If you are not using tiles or a stone, place the baking sheet on the middle rack of the oven. Bake at 500° F. for 15 minutes or until the crusts are golden brown. Sprinkle with the remaining basil and serve each individual pizza on its own plate.

Pizza Rustica

RICOTTA PIE

Even though this pie is known as "rustic pizza" in Italian, it really has very little to do with pizza; it has a top and bottom crust which is slightly sweet and contains no yeast. Serves 4

Ingredients

2 cups unbleached all-purpose flour
2 tablespoons sugar
3 tablespoons chilled butter, cut into small pieces
7 tablespoons chilled lard, cut into small pieces
3 egg yolks
4 whole eggs
1 cup part-skim ricotta
½ pound mozzarella cheese, shredded (use a food processor or cheese grater)
¼ pound provolone cheese, diced
¼ pound salami or prosciutto, diced
½ cup grated pecorino cheese
1 tablespoon chopped fresh Italian parsley
Salt and freshly ground black pepper to taste

Prepare the dough. Sift together the flour and sugar. Cut in the butter and lard with a fork or pastry cutter and blend until the mixture has the texture of cornmeal (you may also use a food processor). Stir in the egg yolks and 1 whole egg until just mixed. Mold the mixture into a ball and chill in the refrigerator for 1 hour.

Preheat the oven to 375° F. Butter and flour a 1½-quart soufflé dish. Divide the dough into two parts, one slightly larger than the other. Roll out the larger part on a floured board. Fold the dough into quarters and transfer it gently to the soufflé dish, unfolding and arranging it to fit against the bottom and partway up the sides of the dish.

In a mixing bowl, stir together the remaining 3 eggs, the ricotta, mozzarella, provolone, salami or prosciutto, grated pecorino, parsley, salt, and pepper. Turn the filling out onto the bottom crust.

Roll out the remaining dough to form the top crust. Press the crust down at the edges to seal well. Bake the pizza in 375° F. oven for 50 minutes, or until the crust is golden brown. Serve at room temperature. It will keep for 24 hours without refrigeration.

Ripieno al Forno

STUFFED CALZONE

With a tossed salad, this Neapolitan "snack" makes a satisfying lunch or supper. Pizza dough folded into a crescent shape encases a savory filling of melted mozzarella, salami, and ricotta. Serves 4

Ingredients

2 recipes Pizza Dough (page 14)
¼ pound salami, chopped
½ pound fresh mozzarella cheese, diced
2 cups part-skim ricotta
¾ cup grated pecorino cheese
Salt and black pepper
Olive oil

Preheat the oven to 500° F. and heat the pizza stone or quarry tiles in the oven for 30 minutes.

Divide the dough into quarters. Roll each quarter out into a circle about 9 inches in diameter.

To make the filling combine the salami, the mozzarella, ricotta, and grated pecorino cheeses, and salt and pepper to taste.

Place one quarter of the filling on one half of a dough round. Fold the dough over to form a half-moon shape. Press the edges of the dough together with your fingers to seal the filling inside. Repeat this procedure with the remaining filling for the other three rounds of dough.

Brush the calzone with olive oil to taste and bake them on the pizza stone or quarry tiles (or use a baking sheet) at 500° F. for 20 minutes or until the crusts are a deep, golden brown. Serve hot.

Opposite: Arancine—Stuffed ▶
Rice Balls (recipe on page 10).
Following page: Four Seasons
Pizza (recipe on page 17).

Uova 'mpriatorio

EGGS IN PURGATORY

This Neapolitan recipe for eggs poached in tomato sauce—not too hotly spiced, since this is only purgatory—makes a nice brunch dish or an easy satisfying supper. Serves 4.

Ingredients

¼ onion, sliced thin
2 tablespoons olive oil
1½ cups peeled, seeded, and chopped tomatoes
2 tablespoons fresh or 2 teaspoons dried basil, chopped or crumbled
Salt and black pepper
4 large eggs

In a 9- or 10-inch skillet, sauté the onion in the oil over medium low heat until it is transparent. Add the tomatoes and the basil and turn the heat up to medium. Simmer for about 10 minutes, until the sauce is thickened, and add salt and pepper to taste.

Break the eggs carefully into the sauce, centering each one on a bed of tomatoes. Cook gently over low heat until the egg whites coagulate. Use a large spoon to place the eggs and the sauce carefully on individual plates.

◀ Opposite: Eggs in Purgatory.
Preceding page: "Thousand Little Things"
Soup (recipe on page 36).

Ova Affucati ca Cucuzzedda

EGGS POACHED WITH SICILIAN SQUASH AND CHEESE

Sicilian squash, featured in this recipe, is like a science-fiction version of zucchini; it is nearly a foot long. You can find it in produce markets in Italian neighborhoods. Once again we have an anthropomorphically named recipe; in the last one the eggs were sent to purgatory, and in this one they "drown" in a panful of squash. Serves 4

Ingredients

1 pound Sicilian squash (about ¼ squash) or zucchini

2 Italian tomatoes, peeled, seeded, and chopped

2 tablespoons fresh or 2 teaspoons dried basil, chopped or crumbled

½ onion, thinly sliced

1 tablespoon chopped fresh Italian parsley

1 clove garlic, minced

¼ cup olive oil

½ cup diced pecorino cheese

4 large eggs

Salt and black pepper

Peel the squash, slice it in half lengthwise, and remove the seeds. Cut it crosswise into thick slices. If you are using zucchini, just cut it into thick slices.

In a large skillet, sauté the squash, tomatoes, basil, onion, parsley, and garlic briefly in the oil. Add 1 cup water, and heat the mixture until it simmers. Cook over medium-low heat until the squash is tender, about 10 minutes.

Sprinkle the pecorino cheese over the mixture and break the whole eggs into the skillet, centering each one on a bed of sauce. Cover the skillet and cook gently until the whites of the eggs coagulate and the cheese melts. Add salt and pepper to taste and serve immediately.

Millassata

SICILIAN FRITTATA

The traditional Italian frittata is a thick omelet that resembles a quiche without a crust. This Sicilian version, with artichokes and asparagus, is full of the tastes of springtime. Beating the egg whites separately makes the frittata high, thick, and light. Serves 4

Ingredients

2 fresh artichokes
Juice of 1 lemon
¾ pound fresh asparagus
6 eggs, separated
3 tablespoons grated pecorino cheese
1 tablespoon chopped fresh Italian parsley
Salt and pepper
2 tablespoons olive oil

Trim off the tough outer leaves of the artichokes, cut off the woody ends of the stems, and scrape out the chokes with a small, sharp knife. In a saucepan, simmer the artichokes, covered, in 1 inch of water with the lemon juice until they are tender, about 20 minutes.

Wash and trim the asparagus and lay it in a skillet. Add water to cover by a few inches and simmer the asparagus until it is barely tender, about 10 minutes. Drain the asparagus and cut it into 2-inch segments.

With a wire whisk, beat the egg yolks with 1 tablespoon of the grated pecorino cheese, the parsley, and salt and pepper to taste. With a wooden spoon gently fold the asparagus and artichokes into the beaten egg yolks.

Beat the egg whites until they are stiff but not dry. Add the remaining cheese to the egg whites and fold this mixture into the yolk-vegetable combination.

Preheat the broiler. Heat the oil in a 10-inch skillet, pour in the egg-vegetable mixture, and cook it over low heat for 20 minutes, until most of the *frittata* has set. Place the skillet under the hot broiler for about 1 minute to cook the top of the frittata, keeping an eye on it to make sure it doesn't burn. Turn the frittata out onto a plate and serve it hot or at room temperature, sliced in wedges.

Frittata di Pasta

PASTA FRITTATA

This is a delicious way to use up leftover pasta (if there ever is any at your house). Some people like this frittata so much that they cook a pot of pasta especially for it. You can use spaghetti, other noodles, or short pasta, and if it's already coated with sauce, that's all the better. If it isn't, be sure to include the onion and anchovies, or the frittata will be too bland. Serves 4

Ingredients

6 eggs
¼ cup grated pecorino cheese
½ pound pasta, cooked al dente
2 anchovies (optional)
1 sliced onion, sautéed (optional)
Salt and pepper
2 tablespoons olive oil
1 tablespoon unsalted butter

Beat the eggs until they are thick. Add the grated cheese and cooked pasta. If you are using leftover pasta with sauce, add the sauce, too. Mash the anchovies with a fork and add them and the sautéed onion to the pasta. Add salt and pepper to taste.

Preheat the broiler. Heat the oil and butter in a heavy skillet until the butter melts and the foam subsides. Pour the egg-pasta mixture into the skillet and cook over low heat for 20 minutes or until the frittata is nearly set. Place the skillet under the hot broiler for about 1 minute to cook the top of the frittata, keeping an eye on it to make sure it doesn't burn. Turn the frittata out onto a plate and serve it hot, sliced in wedges.

Minestre

Minestre

SOUPS

Most Americans regard soup as an appetizer or a light lunch. To the southern Italian peasants, however, a bowl of pasta and beans was often the main meal. When the men went to the fields early in the morning, they often took along bowls of thick bean soup prepared by their wives. Carlo Levi, in his famous book *Christ Stopped at Eboli*, described the evening meal of two poverty-stricken peasants he visited in Basilicata. "Between them they had but one plate and one glass," he wrote. "The plate was full of badly cooked beans, the staple of their meal; sitting at one corner of the uncovered table, mother and son took turns dipping into them with old tin spoons." Life was hard, but the triumph of *la cucina povera* was the transformation of many of these simple dishes (with the addition of wild herbs and a healthy helping of inventiveness) into satisfying, surprisingly tasty meals. Because most people had little meat, many of these soups are based on water, not broth, and are completely vegetarian. Soups prepared for festive occasions did contain both meat and vegetables, however. This chapter includes soups made from practically nothing—like Mariola from Calabria, which is made from sliced frittata—and others like the Millecosedde, an exuberant hodgepodge of favorite southern Italian ingredients.

Sciuscieddu

EGG-BREAD CRUMB SOUP

If you've ever tasted the Roman egg-drop soup called stracciatella and liked it, you'll enjoy this thicker Sicilian version. This is the peasant version of sciuscieddu, which can be made in a matter of minutes; the nobility's recipe is a rich baked dish containing layers of ricotta. Serves 4

Ingredients

1 clove garlic
1 tablespoon fresh Italian parsley
4 large eggs, beaten
2 cups grated pecorino cheese
¾ cup bread crumbs
Salt and pepper
1 quart homemade beef broth or canned chicken broth

Chop the garlic and parsley together to produce a fine homogenous mince. Combine the eggs, grated pecorino cheese, and bread crumbs. Add the garlic-parsley mince and salt and pepper to taste. Mix well with a wooden spoon.

Heat the broth to a simmer. Drop the bread-crumb mixture by spoonfuls into the boiling broth. Cook for 1 minute and serve immediately.

Mariola

SLICED FRITTATA SOUP

You have probably heard the story "Stone Soup," in which visitors hoodwink the townspeople into believing they can make a soup entirely out of stones, if only the townspeople will contribute carrots, meat, celery, and other items. This Calabrian soup is a real example of how to make something out of practically nothing. This skill was highly developed among the poor people of southern Italy, who usually had no choice. Serves 4

Ingredients

4 eggs
1 tablespoon chopped fresh Italian parsley
1 teaspoon dried marjoram
Pinch of salt
½ cup bread crumbs
⅔ cup grated pecorino cheese
Dash of crushed red pepper
2 tablespoons olive oil
1 quart chicken broth, fresh or canned

Beat the eggs well. Stir in the parsley, marjoram, salt, bread crumbs, grated pecorino cheese, and red pepper.

Heat 1 tablespoon of the oil in a 6-inch skillet. Add half the egg mixture and spread it out with a spatula to cover the bottom of the pan. Brown the frittata lightly on one side over low heat. Then turn it and cook the other side. Remove the frittata from the pan (it will be quite thin) and make another one with the remaining olive oil and egg mixture. Cut both frittate into thin ribbons with a sharp knife.

Heat the broth to a simmer. Add the frittata strips and cook for 3 or 4 minutes. Serve immediately.

Zuppa di Ceci

CHICKPEA SOUP

In this thick and satisfying vegetarian soup the onion, tomato, rosemary, and chickpeas blend to produce a flavor that is much more than the sum of its parts. Serves 4

Ingredients

1 pound dried or canned chickpeas
Pinch of salt
1 large onion, sliced
½ cup olive oil
3 tomatoes, peeled, seeded, and chopped
1 teaspoon dried rosemary
Salt and pepper
1 dried hot red pepper, seeded

If you are using dried chickpeas, soak them overnight in water to cover. (If you are using canned chickpeas, start with next step.) Drain and rinse the soaked chickpeas, put them in a kettle with the salt, and add fresh water to cover. Boil them for 1½ hours or until they are tender.

In a very large skillet, sauté the onion in the olive oil until it is golden. Add the tomatoes, rosemary, salt and pepper to taste, and red pepper. Let the mixture simmer for two minutes over medium low heat.

Stir the chickpeas into the skillet and cook for 3 or 4 minutes over medium heat. This soup should be thick, but if it is too thick for your taste, you can add some of the water in which you cooked the chickpeas. Remove the red pepper and serve the soup hot.

Fagioli con il Sedano

WHITE BEAN AND CELERY SOUP

This mild Sicilian soup is very simple to make. The addition of the optional cup of olive oil may puzzle you, but it's not uncommon in southern Italian cooking; often the fruit of the olive tree was the only ingredient available to fortify a soup. Use a fragrant, fruity oil. Serves 4

Ingredients

*½ pound dried cannellini (Great Northern)
beans
2 stalks celery, chopped
2 medium onions, chopped
2 tablespoons olive oil
4 slices Italian bread
1 cup olive oil (optional)
Salt and pepper*

Rinse the beans and soak them overnight in water to cover. Drain the beans, add fresh water to cover by two inches, and boil them for 1½ hours or until they are tender.

Bring two quarts of water to a boil, add the celery, and simmer until the celery can be pierced easily with a fork but is not completely limp.

In a small skillet, sauté the onions in the 2 tablespoons olive oil until they are golden but not brown.

To the pot of beans add the celery with its cooking water and the onions with the 2 tablespoons olive oil. Simmer the soup for about five minutes.

Preheat the broiler. Remove the crusts from the bread and cut it into 1-inch cubes for chunky croutons. Toast them under the broiler for a few minutes, watching carefully to make sure they don't burn.

If desired, add the cup of olive oil to the soup. Sprinkle each serving with salt and several grindings of pepper. Serve the soup hot and pass the croutons.

Minestra di Fagioli e Scarola

ESCAROLE-BEAN SOUP

The escarole in this Neapolitan soup gives it a hint of sweetness. If you like, add a sun-dried tomato or two. Serves 4

Ingredients

1 pound cannellini (Great Northern) beans
1 cup canned peeled tomatoes
2 stalks celery
1 medium onion, chopped
3 tablespoons olive oil
Salt and pepper to taste
1 head (about 1 pound) escarole
2 tablespoons chopped parsley

Soak the beans overnight in water to cover. Drain, add water to cover, and boil for 1 hour or until tender. Add the tomatoes, celery, onion, olive oil, salt, and pepper.

Bring a 5-quart saucepan with salted water to a boil; add the escarole and cover. Heat until the water returns to a boil, then cook for about 10 minutes, or until tender. Drain, squeeze water out of greens, then chop and add to the beans and vegetables. Simmer for 20 minutes. Stir in the chopped parsley and serve.

Minestra di Pomodori e Zucchine

TOMATO-ZUCCHINI SOUP

This simple soup is quick to prepare. If you prefer, you can substitute water for the chicken broth. Serves 4

Ingredients

3 tablespoons olive oil
1 clove garlic
1 tablespoon chopped fresh Italian parsley
2 medium zucchini, trimmed and diced
2 cups peeled tomatoes
Salt and freshly ground black pepper to taste
1/2 teaspoon oregano
3 cups chicken broth

In a 3-quart saucepan, heat the olive oil and sauté the garlic with the parsley until lightly colored. Add the zucchini and sauté for 2 minutes. Add the tomatoes, salt, pepper, and oregano and stir.

Heat the broth until boiling and pour it into the saucepan with the vegetables and seasonings. Simmer, uncovered, over medium low heat for 30 minutes.

Maccu

MASHED FAVA BEAN SOUP

The oldest of all Mediterranean soups, this Sicilian fava gruel served for centuries as the midday meal of peasants, who carried it with them when they went to work in the fields. It consists of nothing more than fava beans, wild fennel (here we offer fresh dill as a substitute), and olive oil, but the taste is surprisingly distinctive. Actually, this soup is not often eaten in Sicily today, because favas were looked down on as a symbol of poverty until the recent revival of *la cucina povera*. My uncle's cousin Maria Serpotta of Catania told me that when she served it at a party, her guests considered it a novelty. Serves 4

Ingredients

1 pound dried fava beans
Pinch of salt
2 sprigs wild fennel or fresh dill
¼ cup rigatoni, penne, or other short pasta
(optional)
4 tablespoons olive oil

Soak the beans overnight in water to cover. Drain them and add fresh water to cover and the pinch of salt. Simmer the beans for 1½ hours or until they are tender, adding the fennel or dill after 45 minutes.

Mash the beans well with a spatula, heavy wooden spoon, or meat mallet.

Cook the pasta al dente, about 10 minutes. Drain and add to the maccu. Stir in the olive oil and serve the soup hot.

Minestra Maritata

MARRIED SOUP

This soup is so called because it is a marriage of meat and vegetables. Different versions are found throughout southern Italy. A variety of greens will produce the most flavorful soup, but if you can't find them all at your market, just use the greens that are available, keeping the proportion between meat and vegetable constant. The soup will still be good. Serves 4

Ingredients

1 bunch broccoli rabe
1 bunch escarole
½ pound Florence fennel (anise) stalks
3 stalks celery
1 head chicory
¼ pound pancetta or salami, sliced
2 tablespoons olive oil
3 cups chicken broth, fresh or canned
1 piece pecorino cheese rind
Salt and pepper
½ cup grated pecorino cheese

Clean the vegetables thoroughly in cool water to remove dirt and sand particles. Remove any damaged sections. Bring a large pot of water to a boil and cook the broccoli rabe until it is just tender, about 10 minutes. Remove the broccoli and simmer the escarole for 10 minutes. Then cook the fennel stalks and celery together for 10 to 15 minutes, and simmer the chicory briefly until it is wilted. Drain the greens and squeeze the liquid out of them. Place them together in a large bowl.

Cut the pancetta or salami into strips and sauté it in the oil. Place the meat, 2 cups of the broth, and the pecorino cheese rind in a large soup kettle. Bring the broth to a boil and let it simmer for 15 minutes. Remove the pecorino cheese rind.

Preheat the oven to 350° F. Place the drained vegetables in layers in an oiled casserole. Sprinkle each layer with salt and pepper to taste, grated pecorino cheese, and a few tablespoons of pancetta with broth. Pour in the remaining cup of broth and bake the minestra in the oven for 20 minutes.

Millecosedde

THOUSAND LITTLE THINGS SOUP

True to its name, this contains just about everything that tastes good in soup—beans, cabbage, onion, pasta, and mushrooms—and the combination lives up to the words food writers always use to describe their favorite soups: "hearty and delicious." Serves 4. Photo 3 following page 20.

Ingredients

¼ pound dried chickpeas
½ head red cabbage
½ pound fresh or 4 ounces dried wild mushrooms
1 onion, chopped
1 stalk celery, chopped
1 carrot, chopped
3 tablespoons olive oil
Salt and black pepper
2 quarts water or chicken broth
¼ pound rigatoni, penne, elbow macaroni, or other short pasta
½ cup grated pecorino cheese

Soak the dried beans overnight in water to cover. Drain. Cut the cabbage vertically into thin slices. If you are using fresh mushrooms, clean and slice them.

In a very large skillet or soup kettle, sauté the onion, celery, and carrot in the oil until they are lightly colored. Add the cabbage and mushrooms, with salt and pepper to taste, and stir. Cook until the cabbage has wilted. Add the beans and water or broth.

Bring the soup to a simmer, and cook it over a low flame for 2 hours, adding the pasta during the last 10 minutes. Serve the soup hot and pass the grated pecorino cheese and a pepper grinder.

Pasta with Green Pepper Sauce ▶
(recipe on page 47).

Primi Piatti

Primi Piatti

PASTA AND GRAINS

Italians sometimes say that theirs is a cuisine of first courses. To be sure, it is in the extraordinary variety of pasta and grain dishes that Italian culinary creativity reaches its peak. That is certainly true in the Mezzogiorno, where a *primo piatto* can be a thousand things other than the spaghetti with tomato sauce you may think of as typically southern.

There is definitive proof that pasta originated somewhere south of Rome long before Marco Polo saw the light of day, let alone traveled to China. Neapolitans and Sicilians have a running battle over who rolled out the first sheet of pasta dough. The people of Bari do not claim to have been the first to make pasta, but they probably deserve to be called its most valiant defenders. In 1647, their Spanish rulers decided to levy a tax on flour and sent their soldiers into homes to check on supplies. The Baresi were furious, and the soldiers' unwanted attentions to the women of their households incensed the people even further. They fought for a solid week until the Spanish gave up.

In this chapter you will find a pasta dish to suit your every mood and to serve on any occasion. At its most festive, pasta may be served with a sauce and stuffed with meat, hard-cooked eggs, cheese, sausages, or a combination of all of these. Lasagne and Cannelloni alla Sorrentina are pasta dishes of this type. At its simplest pasta can be tossed with sautéed vegetables or just boiled in a pot with greens, like Pasta with Broccoli Rabe. Through the centuries exotic ingredients such as raisins, pine nuts, and cinnamon have found their way into traditional Sicilian sauces.

Many of the more elaborate pasta dishes—particularly in Sicily—serve as complete meals *(piatti unici),* not first courses as they are elsewhere in Italy. This is both an Arab legacy and a reflection of the area's historic poverty; combined with pasta, a meager portion of meat or fish flavored with wild mountain fennel or oregano could feed more hungry mouths.

Today, with Americans shifting for health reasons to diets higher in carbohydrates and lower in protein, these time-tested dishes still make sense. If you're trying to limit your cholesterol intake, you'll be glad to learn that although southern Italians are just as fond of egg pasta as we are, they by no means consider it the only kind of noodle worth winding around a fork. Many of the hearty sauces of the Mezzogiorno demand a pasta that will pull its weight—either packaged or homemade with semolina flour and water. Unlike their northern cousins, who favor fettuccine and other noodles, southern Italians are above all devotees of maccheroni—short, factory-made pasta shapes that include ziti, penne, and rigatoni. In Sicily, long hollow noodles called *bucatini* (*il buco* means "hole") are also popular.

The Sicilian use of bread crumbs with pasta may strike you as odd. According to one explanation, this is the Sicilian way of adding texture to pasta with fish sauce while respecting the Italian rule that cheese does not belong in such dishes. Others say that the Sicilians of the past were so poor they could not afford to buy cheese. For the same reason they often extend sauces with nothing richer than hot water from the pasta pot—another boon to dieters.

Rice, which was introduced to Europe by the Arabs in Sicily, did not take hold there except as an ingredient in desserts and in the popular arancine. I have included a delightful modern Catanian creation, Ripiddu Nivicatu, a miniature Mount Etna made of rice and squid. But it is Apulia, the granary of the South, that excels in imaginative rice cooking. Tiella di Patate, Riso, e Cozzi alla Barese, a rice and potato casserole with shellfish, is believed to be a direct descendant of paella, brought by Spanish invaders.

Last but not least among the grain-based dishes are gnocchi, dumplings made of semolina or potato and served with a variety of sauces, and, in Sicily, cuscus, brought by the Arabs and now a specialty of Trapani, where it is steamed in fish broth. Whether you're planning an elegant dinner party or a quick meal after a long day at the office, you'll find a selection of appropriate recipes in this chapter.

Sugo di Pomodoro

TOMATO SAUCE

Preparing tomato sauce from scratch doesn't take much longer than heating up the kind that comes in a jar, and the fresh flavor makes it well worth the effort. Serves 4

Ingredients

1 clove garlic, chopped
1 tablespoon chopped onion
1 tablespoon finely chopped carrot
2 tablespoons olive oil
2 cups peeled, seeded, and chopped plum tomatoes

In a heavy skillet, sauté the garlic, onion, and carrot in the oil until the onion is lightly colored. Add the tomatoes and simmer the sauce for 25 minutes.

Spaghetti alla Puttanesca

SPAGHETTI, WHORE'S STYLE

Why the name? Some say because this favorite Neapolitan dish is quick to make, so it could be prepared between customers. Others say because it's spicy. Either way, you'll get the most wonderful flavor by using a fruity olive oil and fresh tomatoes, the way native Neapolitans do. Serves 4

Ingredients

1 clove garlic, minced
2 tablespoons olive oil
2 cups peeled, seeded, and chopped tomatoes
Salt and black pepper
¼ teaspoon crushed red pepper
1 tablespoon chopped fresh Italian parsley
1 teaspoon oregano
1 pound spaghetti or vermicelli
2 anchovy filets
2 tablespoons capers
8 black olives, pitted

In a heavy skillet, sauté the garlic in the oil until it is lightly colored. Add the tomatoes, salt and pepper to taste, and red pepper. Cook the mixture over medium heat for 3 or 4 minutes, until the tomato liquid is slightly reduced.

Lower the heat, add the parsley and oregano, and simmer the sauce gently for 30 minutes.

Cook the pasta al dente.

Mash the anchovies with a fork and add them and the capers and olives to the skillet. Continue cooking with sauce over low heat until the pasta is ready.

Drain the cooked pasta and toss it with the sauce. Serve hot.

Bucatini alla Carrettiera

BUCATINI, CART DRIVERS' STYLE

If you're partial to eating a wholesome, simple meal at a truck stop on the road, you'll appreciate the Italian counterpart of that kind of fare. In the old days the truckers were horse-drawn-cart drivers who set out in the morning with fresh tomatoes and basil and stopped at lunchtime to boil water for pasta. This meatless dish is quick to prepare and makes an addictive summer supper for backyard gardeners. In Palermo the same name is often given to pasta dressed only with garlic and parsley, but this version is a favorite throughout southern Italy. Serves 4

Ingredients

1⅓ pounds ripe tomatoes (not plum), peeled,
seeded, and chopped
¼ cup chopped fresh basil
2 cloves garlic, minced
¾ teaspoon salt
Black pepper
¼ cup olive oil
1 pound bucatini or perciatelli

In a serving bowl large enough to hold both the sauce and the pasta, combine the tomatoes, basil, garlic, salt, plenty of pepper, and olive oil. Stir the ingredients and set them aside.

Cook the pasta al dente. Drain it, toss it with the sauce, and serve immediately.

Maccaruna i Casa alla Filippino

FILIPPINO'S PASTA SPECIALTY

The restaurant Filippino on the island of Lipari, off Sicily, run by Filippo Bernardi and his descendants since 1910, was once a popular gathering place for anti-Fascist political prisoners exiled to the island by Mussolini. Today it attracts European vacationers who voluntarily flock to Lipari to soak up the sun and enjoy original dishes like this heavenly pasta creation, which shows off some of Sicily's prize ingredients. This recipe makes enough Bolognese Sauce for a future fettuccine dish—when you are in the mood for northern food—or you can freeze it to use in this recipe again. Serves 4

Bechamel Sauce

¾ cup milk
2 tablespoons unsalted butter
2 tablespoons unbleached flour

Scald the milk over medium heat. Melt the butter over medium low heat. Add the flour and stir it in with a fork until it forms a nut-colored roux.

Add the warm milk to the roux ¼ cup at a time, stirring constantly until the sauce is smooth and thick. Keep the sauce warm.

Bolognese Sauce

3 tablespoons unsalted butter
1 tablespoon olive oil
1 medium onion, chopped
1 carrot, chopped
1 stalk celery, chopped
¼ pound pancetta or bacon, chopped
1 pound lean ground beef
1 cup dry white wine
Salt and black pepper
1 28-ounce can peeled tomatoes, with juice

Melt the butter with the oil in a large, heavy skillet. Add the onion, carrot, and celery and sauté them briefly until colored.

Add the pancetta and ground beef, and cook the mixture over medium high heat, stirring, until the beef loses its raw red color. Add the wine and salt and pepper to taste, and cook the mixture until the wine evaporates.

Reduce the heat to low, stir in the tomatoes, and continue to cook the sauce gently for 2 hours, stirring occasionally.

Assembly

2 small Sicilian eggplants or 1 large
eggplant, diced
¼ cup olive oil
1 thick slice boiled ham, chopped
½ pound fresh mozzarella cheese, diced
½ cup freshly grated Parmesan cheese
2 hard-cooked eggs, chopped
1 pound bucatini or ziti
¼ cup freshly grated ricotta salata or
Parmesan cheese
¼ cup fresh basil, chopped

In a heavy skillet, sauté the diced eggplant in the oil, stirring often, until it is golden.

Pour all the Bechamel Sauce and 2 cups of Bolognese Sauce into a deep saucepan. Add the eggplant, ham, mozzarella cheese, grated Parmesan cheese, and hard-cooked eggs.

Cook the pasta al dente. Drain it well and turn it out into the pan of sauces.

Heat and stir the mixture until the cheese melts. Serve this dish garnished with ricotta salata and basil.

Spaghetti con le Zucchine Fritte

SPAGHETTI WITH FRIED ZUCCHINI

Virtually any vegetable can serve as a dressing for pasta. It takes only a few minutes to fry zucchini slices and toss them with spaghetti and cheese, and you've got a surprisingly tasty supper. Serves 4

Ingredients

2 garlic cloves
¼ cup olive oil
4 small zucchini, thinly sliced
Salt and black pepper
1 pound spaghetti
2 cups grated pecorino cheese with peppercorns or ricotta salata

In a large skillet, sauté the garlic cloves in the oil until they are golden and then discard them. Add the zucchini slices to the skillet and sauté them on both sides until they are golden. Add salt and pepper to taste and set the zucchini aside, keeping them warm.

Cook the pasta al dente. Drain it, stir it into the zucchini pan, and toss it with the grated cheese, plenty of pepper, and a few tablespoons of the pasta cooking water.

Maccheroni con Salsa di Peperoni

PASTA WITH GREEN PEPPER SAUCE

This very simple Neapolitan dish adds up to much more than the sum of its parts; the roast peppers impart their sweetness to the sauce, a nice change of pace from "ordinary" tomato sauce. Serves 4. Photo opposite page 36.

Ingredients

3 green Italian peppers
1 clove garlic
2 tablespoons olive oil
1 cup peeled, seeded, and chopped tomatoes
Hot pepper flakes
Salt
1 pound rigatoni, ziti, or other short pasta
2 tablespoons chopped fresh basil

To peel the peppers, first put them under the broiler or place them on a wooden-handled fork and hold them over an open flame until they are blackened on all sides; then hold them under cold running water and peel off the skins with your fingers. Cut the peppers into strips.

In a large, heavy skillet, sauté the garlic clove in the oil until it is golden brown and then discard it. Add the pepper strips, tomatoes, and hot pepper and salt to taste. Simmer the mixture gently for 25 minutes, stirring occasionally.

Cook the pasta al dente. Drain it well, combine it with the sauce and basil leaves, and serve immediately.

Spaghetti con i Funghi

SPAGHETTI WITH MUSHROOMS

You can vary this Neapolitan elaboration of the popular spaghetti with garlic and oil by using any fresh vegetable you may have on hand in place of the sliced mushrooms. Serves 4

Ingredients

1 clove garlic, minced
½ cup olive oil
½ pound mushrooms, sliced
1 pound spaghetti
2 tablespoons chopped Italian parsley
Salt and black pepper
Freshly grated pecorino cheese

In a large skillet, sauté the garlic in oil until it is transparent. Add the mushrooms and sauté them until they are fragrant and moist.

Cook the pasta al dente. Drain it well.

Add the spaghetti to the skillet along with the parsley and salt and pepper to taste and toss the mixture briefly over low heat. Pass plenty of grated pecorino cheese at the table.

Spaghetti Aglio Olio e Peperoncino

SPAGHETTI WITH GARLIC, OIL, AND HOT PEPPER

Some recipes for this popular, simple dish call for charring the garlic cloves in the oil and then discarding them, but this recipe follows the school of thought that cooking them only till golden and leaving them in the sauce results in a wonderful, not at all bitter garlicky taste. Adding water from the pasta pot is a traditional way of extending the sauce. Serves 4

Ingredients

3 cloves garlic, crushed
½ red chili pepper or ½ teaspoon red pepper flakes
¾ cup olive oil
1 pound spaghetti
1 tablespoon chopped fresh Italian parsley

In a large skillet, sauté the garlic and pepper or pepper flakes in the oil until the garlic is pale gold.

Cook the spaghetti al dente. Add 2 tablespoons of the pasta cooking water to the oil-garlic mixture.

Drain the spaghetti and stir it into the skillet with the garlic and oil. Add the parsley, toss briefly, and serve immediately.

Fusilli col tonno

FUSILLI WITH TUNA

Pasta with tuna and tomato sauce has become increasingly popular in the United States. This dish, without the tomatoes, is equally delicious and even easier to prepare. Serves 4

Ingredients

1 pound fusilli
Salt
¼ cup olive oil
1 small onion, chopped
1 6½-ounce can light tuna packed in oil,
drained
2 tablespoons chopped fresh basil leaves
Freshly grated black pepper to taste

Bring a large pot of water to boil, add salt, and put in the pasta.

Meanwhile, heat the olive oil in a medium skillet and sauté the onion until transparent. Reduce the heat to low, add the tuna, and stir for 2 to 3 minutes. Add the basil and remove from heat.

Drain the pasta, add to the skillet, and stir well with the tuna mixture. Season with pepper and serve.

Rigatoni Pomodoro e Ricotta

SHORT PASTA WITH TOMATO SAUCE AND RICOTTA

This simple meatless pasta dish is a comforting combination of ricotta and tomatoes familiar to many Americans of Italian descent. It may well be the quickest pasta dish of all to prepare. Serves 4

Ingredients

1 pound rigatoni, penne, or other short pasta
1 recipe Tomato Sauce (page 41)
½ pound part-skim ricotta
2 tablespoons chopped fresh basil
¼ cup freshly grated pecorino cheese

Heat a large pot of water to a boil, add salt, and cook the pasta al dente. Drain it well. Heat the Tomato Sauce in a saucepan.

Place the ricotta in a large serving bowl, add 1 tablespoon of the Tomato Sauce, and stir. Turn the pasta out into the ricotta-sauce mixture and toss to coat the pasta. Add the rest of the Tomato Sauce and the basil and toss. Serve immediately, passing the pecorino cheese at the table.

Pasta con i Broccoli di Rabe

PASTA WITH BROCCOLI RABE

T he vegetable and pasta are boiled together in the same pot and seasoned with sautéed garlic and anchovies. Serves 4

Ingredients

1 pound penne, rigatoni, or other short pasta
1 pound broccoli rabe, rinsed and trimmed
1 clove garlic, minced
1 dried red pepper, seeded
1 tablespoon olive oil
2 anchovy filets
Salt and black pepper

B ring a large pot of salted water to a boil and add the pasta. Two minutes after the water returns to the boil, add the broccoli rabe. Cook until the pasta is al dente. Drain the pasta and broccoli rabe well.

In a small skillet, sauté the garlic and pepper in the oil. Mash the anchovies with a fork, add them to the skillet, and stir until they dissolve. Remove the skillet from the heat.

Toss the pasta and broccoli rabe with the garlic mixture and add salt and pepper to taste.

Pasta in an Eggplant Shell (recipe on page 58). ▶

Maccheroni con Cavolfiore

PASTA WITH CAULIFLOWER

This is a classic, simple pasta-with-vegetable dish. It's important not to overcook the cauliflower. Serves 4

Ingredients

1 pound cauliflower, cleaned and trimmed
2 anchovy filets
3 tablespoons olive oil
1 pound rigatoni or other short pasta
½ cup grated pecorino cheese
Salt and black pepper

Bring a large pot of salted water to a boil and cook the cauliflower al dente, about 12 minutes. Retrieve the cauliflower with a slotted spoon and reserve the cooking water. Chop the cauliflower into small pieces.

Mash the anchovies with a fork. In a large skillet, sauté the anchovies in the oil briefly. Then add the cauliflower and sauté it briefly.

Cook the pasta al dente in the cauliflower cooking water. Drain it, toss it with the grated pecorino cheese, and combine it with the cauliflower sauce. Add salt and pepper to taste and serve at once.

Pasta con Broccoli

PASTA WITH BROCCOLI

This traditional Sicilian dish is a classic example of delicious sweet-and-sour pasta. The use of saffron is a typical reflection of Arabic influence on the island's cuisine. Serves 4. Photo opposite page 37.

Ingredients

4 tablespoons raisins
Pinch of saffron
3 anchovy filets
2 teaspoons tomato paste
1 head broccoli, florets only
2 cloves garlic, minced
1 tablespoon olive oil
Salt and black pepper
4 tablespoons pine nuts
1 pound bucatini or perciatelli

Soften the raisins in warm water for 15 minutes. Dissolve the saffron in 3 tablespoons hot water. Mash the anchovies with a fork. Dissolve the tomato paste in ¼ cup warm water. Set these ingredients aside.

Blanch the broccoli in salted boiling water for 3 to 4 minutes. Retrieve it with a slotted spoon and reserve the cooking water.

In a large skillet, sauté the garlic in the oil until it is pale gold. Add the anchovies and the tomato-paste solution and cook the mixture for 10 minutes. Chop the broccoli and add it to the skillet with salt and pepper to taste. Cook until the broccoli is tender, about 10 minutes. Stir in the pine nuts, drained raisins, and saffron water.

Cook the pasta al dente in the broccoli cooking water.

Stir the pasta into the skillet with the broccoli and cook over low heat for another 5 minutes. Remove the skillet from the flame, cover it, and let the mixture stand for 5 to 10 minutes before serving. Some Sicilian cooks serve this dish lukewarm; if you prefer it hot, preheat the oven to 425° F. and set the skillet in the oven for 5 minutes before serving.

Pasta Palina

PASTA IN THE STYLE OF THE MONKS OF
SAN FRANCESCO DI PAOLA

These Palermitan monks abstained from meat, but their exotically spiced pasta specialty—fragrant with cloves, cinnamon, and sardines—is almost sinful. Try it with or without cauliflower; the difference in texture makes it seem like two completely different recipes—both delicious. Serves 4

Ingredients

2 pounds cauliflower florets (optional)
2 ounces anchovy filets
1 cup drained, peeled, and seeded tomatoes
1 clove garlic, minced
2 tablespoons chopped onion
¼ pound fresh sardines, cleaned
4 cloves, ground
Dash of cinnamon
3 tablespoons olive oil
1 pound ziti
Pepper

Cook the cauliflower florets in a large pot of salted boiling water for 5 minutes. Retrieve them with a slotted spoon and reserve the cooking water.

Mash the anchovies with a fork and stir them into the tomatoes. In a large, heavy skillet, sauté the garlic, onion, sardines, cloves, cinnamon, and cauliflower in the oil for a few seconds. Turn the heat down to medium low, add the tomato-anchovy mixture and heat it through.

Cook the ziti al dente in the cauliflower cooking water or, if you omit the cauliflower, 5 quarts of salted water. Drain well and toss with the sauce. Pass the pepper grinder at the table.

Pasta con Muddica

PASTA WITH BREAD CRUMBS

Traditionally served in Catania on Good Friday, this rustic dish features fresh sardines, with toasted bread crumbs sprinkled over. Serves 4

Ingredients

2 cups bread crumbs
2 tablespoons tomato paste
3 cloves garlic, chopped
6 tablespoons olive oil
8 fresh sardines, cleaned
2 anchovy filets
Salt
1 pound bucatini or perciatelli

Toast the bread crumbs in a skillet over low heat, stirring continuously, until they are just light brown. Turn them out onto a plate.

Dissolve the tomato paste in ¼ cup warm water. Sauté the garlic in 4 tablespoons of the oil until it is golden, add the sardines and tomato sauce, and cook briefly. The sauce should be liquid.

Sauté the anchovies in the remaining two tablespoons of olive oil. Add them to the sardine sauce.

Cook the pasta al dente, drain it, and toss it with the sauce. Pass the bread crumbs at the table.

Pasta con Sarde

PASTA WITH SARDINES

This dish features fresh sardines. You may substitute the frozen ones imported from Portugal if you are desperate, but avoid canned sardines. Wild mountain fennel grown in Sicily would be ideal, but it is unavailable in this country. Giuliano Bugialli cleverly suggests in his *Classic Techniques of Italian Cooking* that you substitute fresh dill, a closer cousin to the original than the Florence fennel found in American stores. Serves 4

Ingredients

2 tablespoons golden raisins
2 pounds fresh sardines, cleaned
Pinch of saffron
2 cups bread crumbs
2 onions, thinly sliced
½ cup olive oil
4 anchovy filets
2 tablespoons pine nuts
1 pound bucatini or perciatelli
6 sprigs fresh dill or wild fennel

Soften the raisins in warm water to cover for 15 minutes. Clean the sardines and remove the heads, tails, and bones. Dissolve the saffron in 3 tablespoons warm water. Set these ingredients aside.

Toast the bread crumbs in a skillet over low heat, stirring continuously, until they are just light brown. Turn them out onto a plate.

In the skillet, sauté the onions in the oil until they are lightly colored. Stir in the anchovy filets. Add the sardines to the skillet and sauté them for 3 minutes. Then add the drained raisins, pine nuts, and saffron water and turn off the heat.

Cook the pasta al dente, adding the dill or wild fennel to the cooking water. Drain the pasta, retrieve the dill, and add the pasta to the sardine mixture. Chop half the dill and stir it into the pasta-sardine mixture. Cover the skillet and let it stand for 15 minutes. Sicilians are divided into two camps on how this dish should be served—as is or warmed up briefly in the oven (5 minutes at 425° F.).

Pasta 'ncaciata

PASTA IN AN EGGPLANT SHELL

This recipe combines several elements typical of Sicilian gastronomy: eggplant, hard-cooked eggs, and a molded presentation reminiscent of Turkish moussaka. This elegant dish is simple to assemble. Serves 4. Photo opposite page 52.

Ingredients

2 large eggplants, peeled if desired
Salt
1/4 cup vegetable oil
1 pound ziti
1 1/2 pounds tomatoes, peeled, seeded, and chopped
1/2 pound mozzarella cheese, diced
2 hard-cooked eggs, chopped
1/2 cup freshly grated Parmesan cheese
Salt and black pepper

Cut the eggplant into thin slices, sprinkle it with salt, weigh it down with a heavy plate or a cast-iron pot cover, and let it stand for 1 hour. Drain and pat dry.

In a 10-inch skillet, sauté the eggplant in the oil until it is golden brown, about 2 minutes on each side. Drain the slices on paper towels.

Cook the ziti al dente, drain it, and combine it with the remaining ingredients except the eggplant, adding salt and pepper to taste.

Preheat the oven to 425° F. Oil a deep 3-quart casserole and line the bottom and sides carefully with the eggplant slices. Spoon the pasta mixture into the casserole, being careful not to dislodge the eggplant slices. Bake the casserole for 20 minutes or until it is heated through. To unmold, carefully turn the casserole upside down on a platter and slip it off the eggplant shell. If any of the eggplant slices stick to the casserole, pull or scrape them off gently and use them to patch up the shell. Serve immediately.

Penne con Melanzane e Mozzarella

PENNE WITH EGGPLANT AND MOZZARELLA

This dish, also known as Penne alla Sorrentina—Sorrento, near Naples, often lends its name to dishes containing mozzarella—is one of the simplest of pasta creations. Made with fresh basil and tomatoes and snow-white mozzarella, it can also be one of the best. Serves 4

Ingredients

1 pound eggplant, peeled and diced
Salt
4 tablespoons olive oil
1 pound penne
2 cups tomatoes peeled, seeded, and chopped
2 tablespoons chopped fresh basil
½ pound mozzarella, coarsely shredded
Grated pecorino cheese

Sprinkle the eggplant with salt, weigh it down with a heavy plate or a cast-iron pot cover, and let it stand for 1 hour. Drain and pat dry.

In a heavy skillet, sauté the diced eggplant in 3 tablespoons of oil until it is golden on all sides. Drain on paper towels.

Cook the penne al dente and drain it well.

Heat the remaining tablespoon of olive oil in the skillet. Add the penne, eggplant, tomatoes, basil, and mozzarella. Cook the mixture over low heat, stirring constantly, until the mozzarella has melted. Pass the grated cheese at the table.

Pasta alla *Norma*

PASTA WITH EGGPLANT AND TOMATO SAUCE

Catania's pasta specialty is named after the opera *Norma* by the city's favorite son, Vincenzo Bellini. The title has come to be synonymous with "masterpiece." In fact, one tale has it that when the composer was first served this dish he liked it so much that he rather immodestly exclaimed, "This is a *Norma!*" and the name stuck. Serves 4

Ingredients

3 eggplants, peeled and thinly sliced
Salt
½ cup olive oil
1 pound spaghetti or penne
1 recipe Tomato Sauce, heated (page 41)
Grated ricotta salata

Sprinkle the eggplant with salt, weigh it down with a heavy plate or a cast-iron pot cover, and let stand for 1 hour. Drain and pat dry.

Heat the olive oil in a large, heavy skillet and sauté the eggplant until it is golden on both sides. Drain on paper towels.

Cook the pasta al dente, drain, and toss with the Tomato Sauce. Top each serving with eggplant slices and pass the ricotta salata. (Other grated cheeses will suffice, but the dish will not be authentic.)

Pasta e Ceci

PASTA WITH CHICKPEAS

This very simple dish, which resembles a thick soup, is perfect for days when your cupboard is full of assorted nearly empty boxes of pasta. It's important to use a fruity olive oil. Serves 4

Ingredients

1 pound dried chickpeas
¾ cup olive oil
1 tablespoon dried oregano or 2 tablespoons
fresh Italian parsley, chopped
Salt and black pepper
1 pound penne, ziti, rigatoni, broken
fettuccine, or a combination thereof

Soak the dried chickpeas overnight in water to cover. Drain the chickpeas, add fresh water to cover, and simmer them for 1½ hours or until they are tender. (If you use canned chickpeas, place them in a pot with water to cover and go on to next step.)

Add the oil and oregano to the pot of beans and flavor with salt and pepper to taste. If the beans have dried out while cooking, add a small amount of boiling water.

Add the pasta to the bean mixture and cook for 8 minutes. Let stand for 10 minutes or until the pasta is al dente.

Pasta e Fagioli

PASTA WITH BEANS

Long a source of daily nourishment for millions of poor people, this dish makes a satisfying vegetarian supper. Serves 4

Ingredients

½ pound cannellini (Great Northern) beans
½ pound rigatoni, ziti, or other short pasta
½ cup olive oil
3 cloves garlic, minced
1 dried red pepper
1 stalk celery, chopped
1¾ cups tomatoes, peeled, seeded, and chopped
1 teaspoon dried oregano (optional)
Salt and black pepper

Soak the beans overnight in water to cover. Drain and cook the beans in a large pot of simmering water for 1½ hours or until they are tender.

Cook the pasta until it is half done. Heat the oil in a large saucepan and sauté the garlic with the pepper and celery. Add the beans, tomatoes, oregano and salt and pepper to taste and cook the mixture over medium low heat for 5 minutes. Stir in the partly cooked pasta and continue cooking over low heat until it is al dente. Let the mixture stand for 10 minutes before serving.

Lasagne Cacate

The ultimate example of Sicilian culinary humor, this dish takes its name from the appearance of its sauce, made of sausage meat, chopped meat, tomatoes, and ricotta cheese. It is traditionally eaten in Modica, Sicily, on New Year's Day. *"Lasagni cacati e vinu a cannata bon sangu fannu pri tutta l'annata,"* goes the dialect saying, roughly translated as "shitty noodles and plenty of wine bring good health for the whole year." Serves 4

Ingredients

¼ pound stewing beef, in one piece
4 tablespoons olive oil
2 sweet fennel sausages, skinned and chopped
*1 pound tomatoes, peeled, seeded, and
chopped, with their juice*
Black pepper
½ pound part-skim ricotta cheese
*1 pound thin lasagne (about ¾ inch wide) or
wide noodles*
*4 tablespoons grated pecorino cheese or
ricotta salata*

In a large, heavy skillet over medium high heat, brown the beef on all sides in the olive oil. Add the sausage meat and cook, stirring, until brown. Lower the heat, add the tomatoes, and continue cooking for 1 hour or until the meat is tender. Remove the beef, chop it into small pieces, return it to the skillet, and stir it into the sauce.

Grate plenty of black pepper into the ricotta.

Cook the pasta al dente, drain it, and add it to the meat sauce, stirring to coat. Add the ricotta and grated cheese and toss.

Maccheroni Saltati

RIGATONI WITH WINE-BRAISED MEAT

This unusual, very rustic main dish was once served only on special occasions because it contains so much meat. It's hearty, to say the least; one recipe I came across wryly noted that it yielded enough to serve six in Calabria but twice that number in northern Italy. Serves 4

Ingredients

2 pounds pork loin, lamb shoulder, turkey, or
a combination thereof
1 medium-sized onion, sliced
4 scallions, chopped
4 tablespoons olive oil
4 tablespoons lard
2 cups dry red wine
Salt and black pepper
1 pound rigatoni
1 cup freshly grated pecorino cheese

Chop the meat into small pieces. In a large, heavy skillet, sauté the onion and scallions in the oil and lard until they are transparent. Add the meat and sauté it until it is barely brown. Pour in ½ cup of the wine, add salt and pepper to taste, and cover. Simmer over low heat for 1 hour, adding the rest of the wine ½ cup at a time as needed.

Cook the pasta until barely al dente, drain it well, and toss it with the grated pecorino cheese. Add the pasta to the skillet and gently toss it with the sauce for 1 or 2 minutes. Serve in a heated bowl.

Linguine alla Pescatora

LINGUINE, FISHERMAN'S STYLE

This recipe was given to me by Carmela Iuffredo, a young Neapolitan I met in Sicily's Aeolian Islands. Her brother enthusiastically told me that letting the pasta absorb the sauce in individual packets produces "fabulous results." I think you'll agree. Serves 4. Photo opposite page 53.

Ingredients

1 clove garlic, minced
3 tablespoons olive oil
1 pound squid, cleaned (see Techniques) and chopped
2 cups tomatoes, peeled and chopped, with their juice
½ pound mussels (about 1½ dozen)
½ pound littleneck clams (about 1 dozen)
1 pound linguine

In a heavy skillet, sauté the garlic in the oil until it is golden. Add the squid and tomatoes, and simmer for 1 hour. (Many Americans think this is too long a time to cook squid, but that is typical of the Italian technique; the squid's flavor pervades the sauce. If you object, shorten the cooking time.)

Clean the mussels and clams, pry them open with a sharp knife, chop them, add them to the skillet, and cook for 5 minutes.

Preheat the oven to 350° F. Cook the linguine until barely al dente, about 8 minutes. Drain and toss with the sauce. Make 4 serving-sized packets out of aluminum foil and spoon one quarter of the pasta with sauce into each one. Fold the ends over to seal the packets well and heat in the oven for 5 minutes.

La Lasagna

NEAPOLITAN-STYLE LASAGNE

This is the familiar hearty Southern version, bulging with sausage, cheeses, and meatballs. With a salad, it is a complete meal. Serves 8. Photo opposite page 68.

Ingredients

1 pound sweet fennel sausages
½ cup red wine
1 recipe Neapolitan Meatballs (page 83)
simmered in Tomato Sauce (page 41) or Ragù
(page 80)
1 pound part-skim ricotta
2 cups grated pecorino cheese
1 pound lasagne noodles
1 pound fresh mozzarella, sliced

In a heavy skillet, brown the sausages on all sides. Pour in red wine to cover and braise the sausages for 10 minutes or until they are done. Slice the sausages.

Stir 3 tablespoons of the Tomato Sauce or Ragù into the ricotta. Add the grated pecorino cheese and mix well.

Cook the pasta al dente. Retrieve it carefully with two slotted spoons and drain it on paper towels. (Don't stack the lasagne strips; they'll stick together.)

Oil a 9-×-13-inch baking dish. Place one layer of noodles in the pan lengthwise; then crisscross with another layer to build a solid foundation.

Preheat the oven to 425° F. Spoon some meatballs with sauce over the noodles and cover with part of the ricotta mixture. Top with a layer of mozzarella slices and sausage. Crisscross with another layer of pasta and repeat the procedure with the remaining ingredients until they are all used up. Do not let the noodles overlap the sides of the pan; they will turn hard and crunchy during baking.

Bake the lasagne for 30 minutes or until it is bubbly. Let it stand 10 minutes before serving.

Cannelloni alla Sorrentina

CANNELLONI IN THE STYLE OF SORRENTO

Pasta dishes with mozzarella are often dubbed alla Sorrentina, after the picturesque city near Naples that has long attracted Italian and British honeymooners. These cannelloni are relatively light. If you prefer a heartier dish, top them with Ragù (page 80) instead of fresh tomatoes. Serves 4

Ingredients

1½ cups part-skim ricotta
2 large eggs
¾ pounds mozzarella cheese, diced
2 ounces prosciutto, finely chopped
Salt and black pepper
1 recipe 2-egg pasta, rolled out into translucent 4-×-5-inch sheets
1 cup peeled, seeded, and chopped fresh Italian plum tomatoes
¾ cup grated Parmesan cheese

In a medium-sized bowl, combine the ricotta, eggs, mozzarella, proscuitto, and salt and pepper to taste. Stir to make a paste.

Cook the pasta until barely al dente and retrieve it carefully with two slotted spoons. Drain the pasta and carefully spread the sheets out on a damp towel.

Preheat the oven to 350° F. Put two tablespoons of the ricotta mixture on one end of each sheet of pasta and, beginning at the filled end, roll the sheet into a cylinder.

Spread half of the tomatoes in an 8-×-13-inch baking dish. Arrange the cannelloni in the dish and top them with the remaining tomatoes. Sprinkle the grated Parmesan cheese over the top.

Bake the cannelloni for 20 minutes until they are lightly golden on top.

Maccheroni al Forno

BAKED ZITI

This Neapolitan version of the dish can also be made with Ragù (page 80), but this recipe, which contains meatballs, is simpler. It is important not to overcook the pasta or it will turn to mush in the oven. Serves 4

Ingredients

½ pound lean ground beef
1 egg, beaten
2 tablespoons dry bread crumbs
1 onion, chopped
3 tablespoons olive oil
½ cup dry red wine
1 28-ounce can plum tomatoes, with juice
*1 tablespoon chopped fresh basil or 1
teaspoon dried*
1 pound ziti
½ cup freshly grated pecorino
½ pound part-skim ricotta
½ pound mozzarella, diced

To make the meatballs, combine the ground beef, egg, bread crumbs, and onion with a fork. Without packing too tightly, form spoonfuls of meat with your fingers into balls about 2 inches in diameter, rolling them between your palms to make them round.

Heat the oil in a large skillet and brown the meatballs on all sides. Pour in the red wine, reduce the heat to low, and cook for 10 minutes.

Add the tomatoes and basil to the pan and simmer for 20 minutes. Remove the meatballs from the sauce and reserve.

Meanwhile, cook the ziti in a large pot of salted boiling water until very al dente—too firm to the bite. Drain and toss with 1 tablespoon of pecorino and 4 tablespoons of the sauce.

In an ovenproof casserole layer a third of the remaining sauce, the pasta, half the ricotta, a third of the mozzarella, half the meatballs, and a third of the pecorino. Repeat. Finish with a layer of the mozzarella, sauce, and pecorino.

Preheat the oven to 425° F. and bake for 20 minutes, until the top is lightly golden.

Opposite: Neapolitan-style Lasagne ▶
(recipe on page 66).
Following page: Apulian Mussels, Rice, &
Potato Casserole (recipe on page 72).

Risotto alla Posillipo

SHELLFISH RISOTTO

This delicate pink risotto, also known as Risotto alla Pescatora, is served not only in Posillipo, the seaside town near Naples, but in "the city in the sun" as well. Serves 4

Ingredients

2 cloves garlic, chopped
8 tablespoons olive oil
1½ cups peeled, seeded, and chopped fresh
or canned imported Italian tomatoes
1 pound mussels, scrubbed and debearded
1 pound littleneck clams, scrubbed
¼ pound shrimp, shelled
Salt
1 pound squid
1 tablespoon unsalted butter
1½ cups short-grained Italian rice
2 tablespoons chopped fresh Italian parsley

In a heavy saucepan, sauté the garlic in 2 tablespoons of the oil until it is lightly colored. Add the tomatoes and cook over low heat for 10 minutes.

Place the mussels in a saucepan with 1 tablespoon of the oil. Cover the pan and steam the mussels over medium high heat until the shells open, about 5 minutes. Steam the clams in 1 tablespoon of the oil until the shells open. Reserve the clam liquor. Shell the mussels and clams. Cook the shrimp briefly in very salty water until they turn pink.

Clean the squid (see Techniques), chop the tentacles, and slice the body into rings. Sauté the squid in 2 tablespoons of the oil for 15 to 20 minutes.

In a heavy saucepan, heat the remaining 2 tablespoons olive oil with the butter until the butter melts. Add the rice and stir until the liquid is absorbed. In a separate saucepan, bring 1½ cups water to a boil. Cook the rice, adding the boiling water and clam liquor ½ cup at a time, stirring with each addition until the liquid is absorbed.

When the rice is tender and creamy, stir in the tomato sauce, shellfish, and parsley, and serve.

◀ *Opposite: Braciole—meat rolls*
(recipe on page 82).
Preceding page: Couscous Trapani Style
(recipe on page 74).

Riso al Forno

BAKED RICE CASSEROLE

Rice came to Europe from the East via Sicily, but few main dishes based on rice appear in traditional Sicilian cuisine. This unusual *piatto unico,* with a sweet-and-sour meat filling, is an outstanding and hearty exception. Serves 4

Ingredients

1 clove garlic
¼ cup olive oil
1 pound loin veal chops
½ pound tomato puree
½ teaspoon sugar
1 tablespoon pine nuts
1 tablespoon raisins
1¼ cups rice
1 teaspoon salt
3 hard-cooked eggs, chopped
1 ⅔ cups unseasoned bread crumbs
½ cup grated pecorino cheese
¼ pound prosciutto, thinly sliced
½ pound fresh mozzarella cheese, diced
1 tablespoon unsalted butter

In a heavy skillet, brown the garlic in the oil and discard the clove. Add the veal chops to the skillet and brown them on both sides. Dissolve the tomato puree in ⅓ cup water, add it to the skillet, and simmer gently for 40 minutes or until the meat is tender, adding water as necessary.

Remove the meat, chop it into 1-inch cubes, and return it to the skillet. Add the sugar, pine nuts, and raisins and cook for 5 minutes over very low heat until the raisins are plump.

Place the rice in a saucepan with the salt and 2½ cups water, and bring to a boil. Stir the rice and simmer it gently, covered, for 20 minutes or until it is tender.

Preheat the oven to 425° F. Mix the rice with the hard-cooked eggs, 1 cup of the bread crumbs, and the grated pecorino cheese.

Oil a deep casserole and line it with ⅓ cup bread crumbs. Place half the rice mixture in the bottom. Add the prosciutto, then the meat mixture and the mozzarella, and cover with the rest of the rice. Top with the remaining ⅓ cup bread crumbs and dot with the butter. Bake the casserole for 20 minutes or until the top is golden.

Ripiddu Nivicatu

SNOW-CAPPED MOUNT ETNA

A miniature Mount Etna made of rice blackened with squid ink and topped with a snowy peak of ricotta erupting with fiery tomato sauce, this elaborate dish is the creation of Giuseppe La Rosa, founder of Catania's La Siciliana restaurant, today run by his son Salvatore. The best news about this showstopper? It's amazingly simple to make. Serves 4

Ingredients

1 large onion, chopped
4 tablespoons olive oil
1 pound squid
½ cup dry white wine
Salt and black pepper
1 cup rice
½ cup fresh part-skim ricotta
2 tablespoons tomato paste
2 tablespoons Tabasco sauce

In a heavy skillet, sauté the onion in 3 tablespoons of the oil until it is lightly colored. Clean the squid (see Techniques), reserving the ink sacs; chop it and add to the skillet; cook for 5 minutes. Pour in the wine and filter the squid ink into the skillet by mashing the sacs against a sieve with a spoon. Cook the squid for 2 hours, adding water as necessary. Add salt and pepper to taste. Combine the rice with 2 cups of water and simmer for 20 minutes or until all the water has been absorbed.

Force the ricotta through a sieve to make it very smooth.

Combine the rice with the inky squid. On a platter, mold the black rice into a mountain. Flatten the "peak" slightly and top with sieved ricotta to form a snowcap. Make a "fiery eruption" by stirring together the tomato paste, Tabasco sauce, and the remaining 1 tablespoon of oil and spooning it to form a stream of lava. Serve hot, taking care to put a little mountain, snow, and lava on each plate.

Tiella di Patate, Riso, e Cozze alla Barese

APULIAN MUSSELS, RICE, AND POTATO CASSEROLE

A tiella is a traditional Apulian casserole of rice, potatoes, and other ingredients—vegetables or fish. The ancestry of this dish can be traced to paella, the chicken, rice, and shellfish combination introduced to southern Italy by Spanish invaders. Serves 4. Photo 2 following page 68.

Ingredients

2 pounds mussels, scrubbed and debearded
1 clove garlic, minced
1 pound potatoes, peeled and very thinly sliced
Black pepper
1 medium onion
2 tablespoons fresh parsley
1⅓ cups rice

Place the mussels in a saucepan with the garlic and 1 tablespoon water. Cover the pan and steam the mussels over low heat until the shells open, about 5 minutes. Drain the mussels and discard the shells. Filter the liquid and reserve it.

Preheat the oven to 350° F. Place half of the potatoes in a large oiled casserole, seasoning with plenty of pepper. Chop the onion and parsley together to make a homogenous mince and sprinkle half of the mixture over the potatoes. One layer at a time, add the rice, mussels, remaining potatoes, and remaining onion-parsley mince. Grind pepper generously over the top, and pour in enough water to cover, about 3½ quarts. Bake the tiella for 45 minutes or until the rice is tender.

Gnocchi

POTATO DUMPLINGS

These Neapolitan dumplings are also known as *strangolapreti,* or priest stranglers, because according to legend a priest who liked them gobbled them up so fast that he choked. They are usually served with ragù. Serves 4

Ingredients

2 pounds potatoes, peeled and quartered
1 large egg
1 tablespoon olive oil
Salt
1½ to 1¾ cups flour
Additional flour to dust over dumplings

Cook the potatoes in a large pot of salted water for about 20 minutes or until cooked. While they are still hot, pass them through a sieve or ricer. Then let them cool.

Use a wooden spoon to combine the riced potatoes, egg, oil, and salt to taste. Stir in enough flour to form a dough that is soft but not sticky.

Pull off a chunk of dough about the size of your fist and roll it into a long cylinder as thick as your finger. Cut the roll of dough into segments, each about 1 inch long.

Coat your hands, each cylinder of dough, and the work surface with flour. Now you are ready to form the gnocchi into the crescent shape that hastens cooking and holds the sauce. Hold a dough cylinder in the palm of your hand and press it gently against the back of a fork with one finger to form an indentation in the center.

Cook the gnocchi in a large pot of boiling salted water. About 10 seconds after they float to the surface retrieve them with a large slotted spoon. Toss them gently with melted butter and cheese or with Ragù (page 80).

Cuscus

COUSCOUS TRAPANI STYLE

Trapani's specialty is a classic example of Arab-Sicilian cooking. The couscous is steamed in fish broth. The flavor of this very simple dish depends entirely on the richness of the broth, which in turn depends on the flavors and variety of fish used to make it. You can embellish this plain version with steamed mussels or other shellfish. Like Middle Eastern couscous, this can be prepared in the traditional two-level pan that Sicilians call the *cuscusiera* or, lacking that, you can line a sieve with cheesecloth and place it in a saucepan. The steam from the fish broth in the saucepan will cook the couscous in the sieve. Serves 4. Photo 3 following page 68.

Ingredients

½ onion, thinly sliced
3 tablespoons olive oil
2 cloves garlic
1 tablespoon fresh parsley
1 stalk celery
2 tablespoons chopped fresh basil
3 tomatoes peeled, seeded, and chopped
3 pounds fish: a combination of porgy, halibut, whiting, or any similar fish
Salt and black pepper
3 quarts boiling water
1 pound packaged couscous

Heat the oil in a large, heavy saucepan; sauté the onion in 2 tablespoons of the oil until it is transparent. Add the garlic, parsley, celery, basil, and tomatoes, and sauté 5 minutes longer. Add the fish, salt and pepper to taste, and pour in the boiling water. Simmer the mixture gently over low heat for 30 minutes.

Strain the broth and discard the fish. Place half the broth in the lower pan of a *cuscusiera* or saucepan. Put the couscous in the upper pan or in a sieve or steamer lined with cheesecloth and set it into the saucepan. Sprinkle with 1 tablespoon olive oil. Steam the couscous over the simmering broth for 1½ hours, fluffing it up occasionally with a fork.

Reheat the remaining broth. Put the couscous in a bowl and pour in half the remaining broth. Cover and let stand 15 minutes. Stir in the remaining broth, add salt and pepper to taste, and serve.

Carne e Pesce

Carne e Pesce

MEAT AND FISH

The Italian *secondo piatto,* or second course, is frequently austere, for a number of reasons: as its name indicates, it is preceded by a first course, usually pasta or rice; meat has never been plentiful; and fish is usually enjoyed in as natural and fresh a state as possible. In the Mezzogiorno, despite such traditions as the centuries-old Trapanese tuna hunt, the *mattanza,* even whole fish were beyond the means of most people. Yet austerity is not the style of the southern Italian cook. If you enjoy Braciole—the pounded pork or beef rolls stuffed with cheese, raisins, and pine nuts—or Zuppa di Pesce, then you already know how ingenious and satisfying their traditional meat and fish preparations can be. On the following pages you'll discover other time-honored favorites such as Carne alla Pizzaiola, which takes hardly more than ten minutes to make; Sweet and Sour Meatballs from Sicily; and Apulian-Style Fish, baked with potatoes and grated cheese.

Many of the recipes in this chapter are more elaborate than the typical Italian *secondo piatto* because of a quirk of history. Thanks to the influence of their Arab conquerors, Sicilians often serve meat and fish as part of a *piatto unico,* or one-dish meal not preceded by a first course. Recipes such as the Emir of Catania's Chicken Casserole and Salami Ricotta Pie stand beautifully on their own.

Canni c' a' Citu

STEAK WITH VINEGAR

The original recipe, given to me by Chef Pasqualino Giudice of Siracusa, calls for wild oregano, not available here, but domestic oregano will suffice. Although steak did not often find its way to the tables of most Sicilian families, there are several traditional ways to prepare it. Pasqualino and his family, who began by running a butcher shop, prepare steak in their award-winning Ristorante Jonico 'a Rutta 'e Ciauli. Serves 4

Ingredients

2 cloves garlic, crushed
2 tablespoons olive oil
1 pound beef round, thinly sliced
2 tablespoons wine vinegar
1 tablespoon oregano
Salt and black pepper

In a skillet, sauté the garlic in the oil until it is golden. Discard the cloves.

Add the beef to the skillet and brown it on both sides over high heat. Sprinkle the meat with the vinegar, oregano, and salt and pepper to taste. Cover and cook over low heat for 2 minutes longer to let the meat absorb the flavors. Serve immediately.

Spiedini alla Siciliana

GRILLED SCALOPPINE SICILIAN STYLE

These Sicilian veal rolls are stuffed with the same mixture you will use for the Sweet-and-Sour Stuffed Grilled Swordfish (page 102). They're a change of pace for the barbecue grill. Serves 4

Ingredients

¾ cup bread crumbs
2 tablespoons and ¼ cup olive oil
⅛ pound caciocavallo or mozzarella cheese, diced
2 tablespoons grated pecorino cheese
¼ cup pine nuts
1 tablespoon golden raisins
Salt and black pepper
1 pound veal scallops, pounded thin
Bay leaves
1 onion, quartered

Sauté the bread crumbs lightly in the 2 tablespoons olive oil. Mix with the cheeses, pine nuts, raisins, and salt and pepper to taste.

Preheat the broiler. Brush the veal scallops with olive oil and coat them with the bread-crumb mixture. Starting on a short end, roll up the meat slices. Thread one roll on a skewer, followed by a bay leaf, an onion slice, and another veal roll. Repeat until all the meat is skewered. Grill or broil the rolls for ten minutes, turning to brown all sides.

Ragù Napoletano

NEAPOLITAN MEAT SAUCE

Ragù—the cooking, tasting, even the smelling of it—is almost a religious experience for the true Neapolitan. There have even been poems written in its honor. Ragù is not really a tomato sauce but a meat gravy enriched with tomato. Reddish brown, it is used to dress pasta or gnocchi, or as part of lasagne. The flavorful stewed meat is sliced and served as a second course. Ragù is used by the spoonful to season a variety of dishes. Serves 4

Ingredients

2 large onions, chopped
1 tablespoon olive oil or lard
1 pound stewing beef or pork, in one piece
¹/₄ pound prosciutto or pancetta
1 cup dry red wine
1 6-ounce can tomato paste
1 cup homemade beef broth, canned chicken broth, or water

In a deep, heavy skillet, sauté the onions in the oil until they are transparent. Add the beef or pork and prosciutto and brown them over medium heat. Add the wine and cook the meat slowly for about 2 hours.

Dissolve the tomato paste in ½ cup water and stir 2 tablespoons of the mixture into the skillet. Add the remainder of the tomato paste 2 tablespoons at a time, continuing to cook until the sauce is dark, about 2 more hours.

Remove the meat from the skillet and reserve. (Wrap it and put it in the refrigerator.) Continue cooking the sauce over very low heat for another 2 hours, adding broth or water as necessary.

Ragù is best made a day in advance. Let it cool and skim off the fat. Reheat it over a low flame and serve with pasta. Serve the meat separately as a *secondo piatto*, returning it to the sauce briefly to heat up and soak in the flavor.

Carne alla Pizzaiola

MEAT, PIZZA-MAKER'S STYLE

I learned this traditional recipe from my Neapolitan graduate-school classmate Vittorio Felaco, who is today not a pizza maker but a university professor. While the meat is browning, it absorbs the tomatoes, which lightly glaze it. Serves 4

Ingredients

4 cloves garlic
¼ cup olive oil
1½ pounds beef round, sliced across the grain
1½ cups peeled and chopped, imported Italian tomatoes, with their juice
2 teaspoons oregano
Salt and black pepper

In a heavy skillet, sauté the garlic in the oil until it is golden. Add the meat to the skillet, top it with the tomatoes and their juice, sprinkle the oregano over it, and add salt and pepper to taste. Cook over medium high heat for 10 minutes, stirring once until the meat is lightly browned and glazed. Discard the garlic and serve.

Braciole

PORK OR BEEF ROLLS

Unlike the grilled Spiedini alla Siciliana (page 79), these meat rolls are braised in a tomato sauce to which they impart a wonderful rich flavor. Serves 4. Photo 4 following page 68.

Ingredients

1 tablespoon raisins
1 pound boneless pork loin or beef round,
thinly sliced
¼ pound prosciutto, chopped
¼ cup grated Parmesan or pecorino cheese
1 tablespoon pine nuts
1 clove garlic
2 tablespoons olive oil
2 tablespoons tomato paste
½ pound tomatoes with their juice
Salt and black pepper

Soak the raisins in warm water to cover for 30 minutes. Pound the pork or beef slices until they are thin.

Mix together the chopped prosciutto, grated cheese, pine nuts, and drained raisins. Spread the mixture on the meat slices and roll them up. Secure each roll with twine or a toothpick.

In a deep, heavy skillet, sauté the garlic in the oil until it is golden and then discard the clove. Add the pork or beef rolls to the skillet and brown them on all sides over medium high heat. Dissolve the tomato paste in 1 cup warm water. Add the tomato-paste mixture to the skillet, along with the tomatoes and their juice. Season with salt and pepper to taste. Lower the heat and simmer, covered, for 45 minutes, turning the braciole occasionally and basting them with the sauce. Serve the sauce with pasta, the meat as a second course.

Polpette alla Napoletana

NEAPOLITAN MEATBALLS

Many Americans are surprised to discover that in Italy meatballs are not served on top of spaghetti. The sauce they are cooked in is served with pasta, and the meatballs are a second course. Serves 4

Ingredients

½ loaf Italian bread, cut into chunks
1 cup milk
1 pound lean ground beef
½ cup grated Parmesan cheese
1 clove garlic, minced
1 teaspoon dried basil
1 teaspoon dried marjoram or oregano
2 large eggs
Pinch of freshly ground nutmeg
Salt and black pepper
¼ cup olive oil
1 recipe Tomato Sauce (page 41)

In a small bowl, soak the bread in the milk for 15 minutes. Squeeze it out and let it drain, reserving the milk. Combine the bread with the ground beef, grated cheese, garlic, basil, marjoram, milk, eggs, nutmeg, and salt and pepper to taste.

Mold the mixture into balls about the size of lemons. Don't pack it too compactly.

In a large, heavy skillet, brown the meatballs in the oil over high heat, turning them gently and taking care not to crowd them; you may have to brown them in two batches.

Pour off the fat and oil from the pan, lower the heat, and add the Tomato Sauce. Simmer the meatballs gently in the sauce for 10 to 15 minutes.

Polpette all'Agrodolce

SWEET-AND-SOUR MEATBALLS

If you thought only Swedes made sweet-and-sour meatballs, these Sicilian ones will come as a pleasant surprise. Serves 4

Ingredients

1 pound lean ground beef
1 egg
2 tablespoons pine nuts
2 tablespoons raisins
Pinch of cinnamon
Salt and black pepper
2 amaretti cookies
2 tablespoons milk
¼ cup olive oil
2 tablespoons sugar
½ cup white wine vinegar

Mix together the beef, egg, pine nuts, raisins, cinnamon, and salt and pepper to taste. Soak the amaretti in the milk, squeeze them out, and mix them into the meat mixture. Mold the mixture into meatballs about 3 inches in diameter. Don't pack them too compactly.

In a heavy skillet sauté the meatballs in the oil over medium high heat until they are lightly browned. Dissolve the sugar in the vinegar and add it to the skillet. Roll the meatballs around the pan over medium low heat until the vinegar has almost evaporated. Serve the meatballs hot.

Opposite: Lamb Hunter's Style ▶
(recipe on page 86).
Following page: Orange Chicken Catania
Style (recipe on page 88).

Farsumagru

SICILIAN STUFFED BEEF ROLL

Many theories have been propounded in American cookbooks on the meaning of the name *farsumagru,* Sicily's undisputed premier meat dish. To settle the argument, the word means "false lean," because it is a fraudulently simple-looking meat roll whose insides bulge with a rich stuffing of eggs, cheese, meats, and peas. It can be eaten hot or at room temperature. Serves 4.

Ingredients

1 clove garlic, minced
¼ pound lean ground beef
1 egg, beaten
¼ cup soft bread crumbs
3 tablespoons grated pecorino cheese
¼ pound shelled fresh or frozen peas, cooked
2 tablespoons chopped fresh Italian parsley
Salt and black pepper to taste
1½ pounds lean beef or veal in one slice
½ pound salami, chopped
½ pound prosciutto, sliced
3 whole hard-cooked eggs
1 onion, chopped
3 tablespoons olive oil
1 cup red wine
1 tablespoon tomato paste

In a large bowl combine the garlic, ground beef, beaten egg, bread crumbs, grated cheese, peas, parsley, and salt and pepper. Pound the beef or veal slice until it is ⅛ inch thick. Cover the slice with salami and prosciutto and spoon on the ground-beef mixture. Arrange the whole hard-cooked eggs, end to end, along a short end of the beef or veal slice. Starting at that end, carefully roll up the meat slice and secure it with twine.

In a heavy skillet, sauté the onion in the oil over medium high heat until it is transparent. Add the meat roll to the skillet and brown it on all sides.

Pour in the wine and cook over medium heat until the wine evaporates. Dissolve the tomato paste in one cup water and add it to the skillet. Cook slowly over low heat until the meat roll is tender and the sauce reduced, about 1½ hours. Add salt and pepper to taste. Let the farsumagru stand for a few minutes. Serve it, either hot (with the sauce) or at room temperature, in 1-inch-thick slices. Each slice should have at its center a medallion of yellow egg yolk and a few peas.

◀ *Opposite: Farsumagru—Sicilian Stuffed*
Beef Roll
Preceding page: Swordfish Pie
(recipe on pages 104-105).

Agnello alla Cacciatora

LAMB HUNTER'S STYLE

In this simple Apulian dish, as in Irish stew, the lamb is not browned before braising. If you like, prepare it a day in advance and reheat after scraping the fat off the top. Serves 4. Photo opposite page 84.

Ingredients

2 pounds boneless lamb shoulder
$^1/_2$ cup canned or fresh tomatoes, peeled, seeded, and chopped
1 onion, sliced and separated into rings
2 tablespoons minced fresh Italian parsley
1 teaspoon dried oregano
1 dozen green olives, pitted
2 tablespoons olive oil
Salt and black pepper

Preheat the oven to 300° F. Cut the lamb into 1½-inch chunks. Oil a Dutch oven or heavy casserole and place the lamb in it with the tomatoes, onion, parsley, oregano, olives, oil, and salt and pepper to taste. Mix well.

Cover and bake the lamb for 40 minutes. Serve hot.

Costolette di Maiale Ripiene

STUFFED PORK CHOPS

Since these chops, with their bread crumb and cheese filling, are a hearty main course, they're best served with a salad or a simply prepared vegetable. Serves 4

Ingredients

4 ¾-inch-thick loin pork chops
1 large onion, chopped
1 tablespoon olive oil
6 tablespoons soft bread crumbs
1 tablespoon chopped fresh Italian parsley
2 eggs, beaten
4 tablespoons grated Parmesan or pecorino cheese
Pinch of freshly grated nutmeg
Salt and black pepper
Flour for dredging
2 tablespoons butter
3 tablespoons olive oil

Ask your butcher to cut pockets in the pork chops or do it yourself by making a deep horizontal cut along the flat side with a sharp knife.

In a small skillet, sauté the onion in the oil until it is transparent. Add the bread crumbs and parsley and stir over medium heat until the bread crumbs are lightly browned and the onion is golden. In a bowl, combine the bread-crumb mixture with the eggs, grated cheese, nutmeg, and salt and pepper to taste.

Use a teaspoon or demitasse spoon to fill the pockets of the pork chops with the stuffing. Close the pockets and secure them with toothpicks. Dredge the chops in flour.

In a heavy skillet, heat the oil and butter until the butter melts and becomes foamy. When the foam subsides, add the pork chops and brown them on both sides. Lower the heat, cover, and cook the pork for 40 minutes or until it is tender and no longer pink.

Pollo all'Arancia alla Catanese

ORANGE CHICKEN CATANIA STYLE

Chicken is not very popular in Sicily, presumably because the hens are kept for the eggs they produce. But fortunately the cooks of Catania took advantage of the fragrant orange groves that cover their hillsides to come up with this unusual chicken dish. For an intensified, albeit unauthentic, orange taste, substitute Cointreau for the cognac. Serves 4. Photo 2 following page 84.

Ingredients

1 3-pound chicken, cut into pieces
1 clove garlic
1 tablespoon fresh or 1 teaspoon dried rosemary, minced or crumbled
1 tablespoon fresh or 1 teaspoon dried mint, minced or crumbled
1/4 teaspoon freshly grated nutmeg
1 onion, chopped
1/2 cup olive oil
1/2 cup fresh orange juice
4 tablespoons cognac, Sicilian brandy, or Cointreau
1/4 to 1/2 cup chicken broth
Salt and black pepper

Preheat the oven to 400° F. Rub the chicken with the garlic, rosemary, mint, and nutmeg.

In a heavy ovenproof skillet, sauté the chopped onion in the olive oil until it is golden. Add the chicken and brown it on all sides. Lower the heat and add the orange juice and cognac.

Roast the chicken, in the skillet, for 1 to 1½ hours, basting with chicken broth, until it is tender. Add salt and pepper to taste.

Place the chicken on a serving plate. If the sauce is too thin, reduce it over high heat. Pour it over the chicken and serve.

Pollo alla Cacciatora

CHICKEN HUNTER'S STYLE

This Neapolitan version of the popular dish has a distinctively fresh taste because the tomatoes are cooked just briefly. Serves 4

Ingredients

1 onion, sliced
6 tablespoons olive oil
1 chicken, cut into pieces
1 cup dry white wine
2 bay leaves
Salt and black pepper
1 cup peeled and seeded fresh plum tomatoes
¼ cup chopped fresh basil leaves

In a large skillet, sauté the onion in the oil until it is transparent. Add the chicken and brown it on all sides.

Lower the heat to a slow simmer and pour in the wine. Add the bay leaves and salt and pepper to taste. Cover and braise for 40 minutes, turning the chicken once. Add the tomatoes for the last 10 minutes. When the chicken is done, stir in the basil and serve.

Pasticcio di Mohammed ibn Itmnah (Thumma)

THE EMIR OF CATANIA'S CHICKEN CASSEROLE

Just as the Chinese have their thousand-year-old eggs, Sicilians pride themselves on this thousand-year-old chicken. This recipe for chicken with exotic nuts encased in a round bread loaf really is nearly a thousand years old; it dates back to the days when the Arabs still held Sicily and the Emir Mohammed ibn Itmnah ruled Catania. I have drawn it from his original wording without changing a single ingredient. As a rule, I find that historic recipes are often better left in the library, and so I was very pleasantly surprised to discover that this one produces a dish that genuinely tastes good. Serves 4

Ingredients

1 3½-pound chicken cut into 8 parts
¼ cup olive oil
2 cups chicken broth
Salt and black pepper
1 large round loaf crusty Italian bread (not a ring)
⅛ cup toasted almonds
⅛ cup pisachios
1 tablespoon capers
1 tablespoon fresh Italian parsley
2 eggs, beaten
Juice of 1 lemon

In a heavy ovenproof skillet, sauté the chicken in the oil over medium heat until it is brown on all sides. Pour in 1 cup of the broth and add salt and pepper to taste. Cook the chicken over low heat, adding broth as necessary, for 1 hour, until the meat starts to fall off the bones. Pour off the broth and reserve it. Bone the chicken.

Cut the bread in half horizontally and hollow out each half of the crust, reserving the soft insides.

Combine the insides of the bread with the chicken cooking broth and press the mixture through a sieve.

Preheat the oven to 350° F. Grind the almonds, pistachios, capers, and parsley together into very small pieces. The emir's cook probably used a mortar and pestle; you can use a blender or food processor.

Add the nut mixture to the pureed bread and broth, along with the eggs and lemon juice.

Add the boned chicken to the mixture. Stuff the bottom bread crust with it. Cover with the top crust and bake for 20 minutes or until the crust is crisp and the filling is heated through. This is especially good hot, although it may be served at room temperature.

Coniglio in Agrodolce

SWEET-AND-SOUR RABBIT

Rabbit is popular in Sicily and elsewhere in Italy, where many country families raise rabbits in backyard cages. Serves 4

Ingredients

1 onion, chopped
½ cup olive oil
1 rabbit, cut into pieces
Flour for dredging
1 cup white wine vinegar
4 tablespoons sugar
2 bay leaves
Salt and black pepper
2 tablespoons tomato paste
1 tablespoon pine nuts
1 tablespoon raisins
4 stalks celery, chopped
2 tablespoons capers
¼ cup green olives, pitted

In a heavy skillet, sauté the onion in the oil until it is golden, about 5 minutes.

Dredge the rabbit in flour, add it to the skillet, and brown it on all sides. Add the vinegar, sugar, bay leaves, and salt and pepper to taste. Dissolve the tomato paste in ½ cup water and add it to the skillet. Cook over low flame for 20 minutes.

Stir in nuts, raisins, celery, and capers and cook for 20 minutes longer or until the meat is tender. Serve on a heated platter.

Coniglio alla Siciliana

RABBIT SICILIAN STYLE

The rabbit is marinated in wine and herbs, sautéed, and then braised in the marinade. A simple but delicious dish. Serves 4

Ingredients

2 cups dry red wine
1 bay leaf
½ onion
½ stalk celery
1 teaspoon dried sage leaves
1 teaspoon dried rosemary
1 carrot
Black pepper
1 2½-pound rabbit, cut into pieces
¼ cup olive oil
3 tablespoons wine vinegar

In a saucepan, combine the red wine, the bay leaf, onion, celery, sage, rosemary, carrot, and black pepper to taste. Simmer the mixture for 20 minutes. Remove it from the heat. Place the rabbit in a large glass bowl. When the wine mixture has cooled, pour it over the rabbit, cover, and marinate in the refrigerator for 6 hours or overnight. Remove the rabbit, strain the marinade, and reserve it.

In a heavy skillet, sauté the rabbit in the oil until it is golden on all sides. Reduce the heat to low. Sprinkle the rabbit with the vinegar, and when the vinegar has evaporated, add half of the strained marinade to the pan. Cook the rabbit, covered, over low heat for 1 hour, continuing to add marinade until the meat is tender.

Torta di Salame e Ricotta

SALAMI-RICOTTA PIE

This makes a nice lunch or informal supper dish. It is a sort of Mediterranean version of shepherd's pie. For reasons of nutrition I never peel potatoes before I mash them; this recipe turns out fine that way. Serves 4

Ingredients

2 pounds potatoes, scrubbed
3 large eggs
1 tablespoon butter
1 pound part-skim ricotta
Pinch of freshly ground nutmeg
Salt and black pepper
1/2 cup bread crumbs
1/4 pound salami
3 hard-cooked eggs, sliced
2 tablespoons butter

Boil the potatoes in their skins in a large kettle of salted water. Mash them and combine them with the 3 raw eggs, 1 tablespoon butter, ricotta, nutmeg, and salt and pepper to taste.

Preheat the oven to 350° F. Oil a 3-quart casserole and line it with half the bread crumbs. Spoon half the potato mixture into it. Arrange the salami and hard-cooked egg slices on top and cover with the rest of the potato mixture. Sprinkle with the rest of the bread crumbs, and dot with the butter.

Bake the pie for 30 minutes, until the top is puffed and golden brown.

Salsiccia allo Spiedo

SAUSAGE ON A SKEWER

This is a twist on the usual kebab, easy to fix and delicious to eat. Serves 4

Ingredients

1 pound Italian pork sausage
1 loaf day-old Italian bread
Bay leaves
2 tablespoons olive oil

Cut the sausages into 2-inch chunks. Cut the bread into thick slices and quarter the slices.

Thread the ingredients onto skewers in the following order: bread, sausage, bay leaf, sausage, bread, sausage, bay leaf, and so on. Sprinkle with the oil.

Preheat the broiler. On a rack 5 inches from the heat, broil the sausage kebabs for 5 minutes on each side or until the sausage is cooked through.

Scaloppine al Marsala

VEAL MARSALA

In restaurants in the United States, this dish is often heavy and cloying. As prepared in Italy, however, it consists of thin, tender scaloppine with a delicate wine glaze. Serves 4

Ingredients

1½ pounds veal scalops
Flour for dredging
3 tablespoons butter
1 cup Marsala wine
Salt and pepper to taste
2 tablespoons chopped fresh parsley

Pound the veal briefly, taking care not to tear it. Dredge it in flour.

Melt the butter in a large skillet over medium heat, add the veal, and sauté on both sides until golden. Remove the veal from the pan.

Pour the Marsala into the pan to deglaze. Reduce the heat to low, stir 1 tablespoon flour into the wine, and return the veal to the pan, turning to coat with the sauce. Cover and cook over low heat for 5 minutes. Season to taste, sprinkle with chopped parsley, and serve hot.

I Gamberetti 'a Rutta 'e Ciauli

PASQUALINO GIUDICE'S SAUTÉED SHRIMP

This recipe was given to me by Pasqualino Giudice, proprietor of the Ristorante Jonico 'a Rutta 'e Ciauli in Siracusa. The family restaurant has a fascinating collection of traditional kitchenware and decorative breads as well as a wonderful view of the sea. Chef Giudice's passion is keeping authentic Sicilian cooking alive and spreading the good word about it, and he has won awards all over Europe for his achievements. Serves 4. Photo opposite page 100.

Ingredients

3 cloves garlic, sliced thin
3 tablespoons olive oil
1 pound shrimp, shelled and deveined
¾ cup dry white wine
1 stalk celery, blanched and chopped
½ cup Tomato Sauce (page 41)
2 peeled, seeded, and chopped tomatoes
1 teaspoon dried oregano
Salt and black pepper

In a large skillet, sauté the sliced garlic in the oil until it is golden. Add the shrimp, wine, celery, Tomato Sauce, tomatoes, oregano, and salt and pepper to taste. Sauté the shrimp until they turn pink, about 10 minutes.

Cozze Arraganate alla Tarantina

MUSSELS WITH OREGANO IN THE STYLE OF TARANTO

A specialty of Taranto, near Bari, this mussel preparation is simple and tasty. Serves 4

Ingredients

2 tablespoons olive oil
4 pounds mussels, scrubbed and debearded
2 cloves garlic
2 tablespoons fresh Italian parsley
½ cup bread crumbs
6 tomatoes, peeled and chopped
Salt and black pepper
¾ cup dry white wine

Brush a baking pan with 1 tablespoon of the olive oil. Pry open the mussels with an oyster knife. Discard the top shells and arrange the mussels in the pan in their bottom shells.

Chop the garlic and parsley together to form a homogenous mince. Combine with the bread crumbs and sprinkle the mixture over the mussels.

Preheat the oven to 400°F. In a small saucepan, sauté the tomatoes in the remaining tablespoon olive oil for 10 minutes. Add salt and pepper to taste.

Bake the mussels in the oven for 5 minutes. Pour the wine into the baking pan, spoon the tomatoes over the mussels, and increase the heat to 450°F. Bake the mussels 10 minutes longer. Serve hot or at room temperature.

Zuppa de Pesce

FISH SOUP

Although this is called a soup, it is really a thick stew of different kinds of fish that is served all over southern Italy as a main course. Nowhere is it written that you have to use these particular fish; try different mixtures of fish and shellfish. It's the variety that's important. A famous Apulian version called zuppa di pesce alla gallipolina contains squid, jumbo shrimp, and mussels and is believed to have descended from an ancient Spartan soup. Serves 4. Photo opposite page 101.

Ingredients

2 cloves garlic
¼ cup olive oil
1 large onion, chopped
¼ pound squid, cleaned (see Techniques) and chopped
1 cup dry white wine
4 cups peeled and chopped tomatoes, with their juice
4 tablespoons chopped fresh Italian parsley
1 stalk celery, chopped
2 bay leaves
Salt and black pepper
¼ teaspoon crushed red pepper flakes or ½ dried red pepper
½ pound fresh cod filet
1 whole whiting
¼ pound mussels, scrubbed and debearded
6 slices coarse Italian bread

In a cast-iron soup kettle, or deep pot, sauté garlic in oil until golden; discard clove. Add onion and squid, and sauté until colored. Add wine and cook over low heat until it evaporates, about 10 minutes.

Preheat the oven to 250° F. Add the tomatoes, half the parsley, the celery, bay leaves, salt and pepper to taste, red pepper, cod filet, and whiting and cook for a total of 15 minutes. *Do not stir* or the fish will disintegrate. Add the mussels and continue cooking until the shells open. Remove the bay leaves and the dried pepper, if using.

Toast the bread in the oven for 7 minutes. Place 1½ slices of toast in each soup bowl and carefully spoon the soup over them. Garnish with remaining parsley and serve hot.

Pesce alla Pugliese

APULIAN-STYLE FISH

The inclusion of matchstick potatoes distinguishes this Apulian baked-fish recipe, whose flavor is enhanced with a generous topping of freshly grated pecorino cheese. Serves 4

Ingredients

1 clove garlic
1 tablespoon chopped fresh Italian parsley
1½ pounds potatoes, peeled and cut into matchsticks
2 ¾-pound porgies
Salt and black pepper
⅔ cup grated pecorino cheese
3 tablespoons olive oil

Preheat the oven to 350° F. Chop the garlic and parsley together to form a homogenous mince.

Oil a flat roasting pan. Put half the potatoes in the bottom with half the garlic-parsley mince. Arrange the fish on top of the potatoes, add salt and pepper to taste, and top with the rest of the potatoes, the remainder of the garlic-parsley mixture, and the grated cheese. Sprinkle with the olive oil. Bake the casserole for 35 minutes or until the fish flakes when pierced with a fork.

Sautéed Shrimp (recipe on page 97). ▶

Baccalà Fritto

FRIED SALT COD

Baccalà has long been a favorite in Italy for Lent and Christmas Eve. Be sure to pound it before cooking. Serves 4

Ingredients

2 pounds baccalà
Flour for dredging
Olive oil for frying
Juice of 1 lemon

Cover the fish with cold water and let it soften for 12 hours in the refrigerator, changing the water 3 times.

Drain the fish, pat it dry with paper towels, and pull off the skin with your fingers and a sharp knife. Bone the fish and pound it briefly to soften it. Cut it into strips and dredge it in flour.

Pour oil into a skillet to a depth of about ⅛ inch and heat it over a medium high flame. Sauté the fish on both sides until it is golden. Serve it hot or at room temperature with a sprinkling of lemon juice.

Involtini di Pesce Spada

SWEET-AND-SOUR STUFFED GRILLED SWORDFISH

This version of a popular Sicilian recipe was given to me by Francesco Ammirata, a native of Palermo and chef at the Jolly Hotel. It's a terrific change of pace for a barbecue. Serves 4

Ingredients

1 pound swordfish, ¼ inch thick
1 onion, finely chopped
1 tablespoon olive oil
1½ cups bread crumbs
2 anchovy filets
1 clove garlic
2 tablespoons pine nuts
1 tablespoon golden raisins
2 tablespoons grated Parmesan or pecorino cheese
1 tablespoon lemon juice
1 tablespoon orange juice
1 egg, beaten
Salt and black pepper

Cover the swordfish with wax paper and pound it carefully with a meat pounder or the handle of a heavy knife.

In a small saucepan, sauté the chopped onion in the oil until it is transparent. In a medium-sized bowl combine the onion with the bread crumbs, anchovy filets, garlic, pine nuts, raisins, grated cheese, lemon juice, orange juice, beaten egg, and salt and pepper to taste.

Cut the swordfish filets into 5-x-2-inch strips. Spread the filling thinly over each swordfish filet. Roll the filets tightly and secure them with toothpicks.

Coating

1 egg, beaten
1 tablespoon olive oil
1 cup bread crumbs
2 tablespoons grated Parmesan or pecorino cheese
½ teaspoon oregano
1 tablespoon chopped fresh Italian parsley
1 clove garlic, minced
Salt and black pepper
3 large onions, sliced
Bay leaves

Preheat the broiler or light the charcoal grill. Stir the beaten egg and olive oil for the coating together with a fork. In a separate bowl combine the bread crumbs, grated cheese, oregano, parsley, garlic, and salt and pepper to taste. Dip the swordfish rolls in the olive oil-egg mixture and roll them in the bread-crumb mixture to coat lightly. Thread the rolls onto skewers, alternating with sliced onions and bay leaves.

Grill under a hot broiler or on a charcoal grill, 6 inches from the flame, for 10 minutes or until the swordfish rolls are cooked through, basting twice with olive oil.

Impanata di Pesce Spada

SWORDFISH PIE

This pie, whose name derives from the Spanish *empanada* and is undoubtedly a legacy of Spanish invaders, is an elegant package bursting with all the wonderful tastes of Sicily: swordfish, olives, raisins, pine nuts, capers, and more. The marriage of a slightly sweet crust with the fish is unusual and delicious. Serves 4. Photo 3 following page 84.

Ingredients

1 onion, chopped
1 tablespoon olive oil
1 cup drained and peeled tomatoes
½ cup green olives, pitted
½ cup golden raisins
3 tablespoons pine nuts
2 tablespoons capers
2 cups all-purpose unbleached flour
2 tablespoons sugar
3 tablespoons chilled butter, cut into small pieces
7 tablespoons chilled lard, cut into small pieces
3 egg yolks
1 whole egg
Grated rind of 1 orange
1 pound swordfish
½ pound caciovallo or mozzarella cheese, diced
1 egg, beaten

In a heavy skillet, sauté the onion in the oil until it is transparent. Reduce heat to low, add the tomatoes, olives, raisins, pine nuts, and capers, and cook for 5 minutes. Set aside.

Prepare the dough. Sift together the flour and sugar. Cut in the butter and lard with a fork or pastry cutter and blend until the mixture has the texture of cornmeal. Stir in the egg yolks, whole egg, and orange rind until just mixed. Mold the mixture into a ball and chill it in the refrigerator for 1 hour.

Divide the dough into two parts, making one part twice as big as the other. Roll out the larger part on a floured board. Fold the dough into quarters and transfer it gently to a 9-inch pie pan, unfolding and arranging it to fit the pan.

Preheat the oven to 350°F. Cut the fish into chunks and arrange them on the bottom crust. Sprinkle with the tomato mixture and top with the diced cheese.

Roll out the remaining dough to form the top crust. Place it on the pie and cut two vents in it to allow steam to escape. Brush with the beaten egg. Bake the pie for 50 minutes, or until the crust is golden brown. Serve hot.

Sarde a Beccaficu alla Palermitana

SWEET-AND-SOUR SARDINES PALERMO STYLE

These fresh sardines, stuffed with a sweet-and-sour mixture, are named for the beccafico, a bird that eats ripe figs and is therefore considered a gourmand. This is one of Italy's most famous dishes. Serves 4

Ingredients

1 pound fresh sardines
½ cup dry bread crumbs
1 tablespoon olive oil
1 clove garlic, minced
1 tablespoon golden raisins
1 tablespoon pine nuts
1 tablespoon freshly grated pecorino cheese
1 tablespoon chopped fresh Italian parsley
Salt and black pepper
Bay leaves
½ teaspoon sugar
Juice of 1 lemon

Clean the sardines. Remove the heads and backbones but leave the tails intact. Cut them open lengthwise, rinse, and pat dry with paper towels.

Sauté the bread crumbs lightly in the olive oil, stirring constantly.

Combine half of the bread crumbs with the garlic, raisins, pine nuts, grated pecorino cheese, parsley, and salt and pepper to taste. Spread the mixture on the cut side of one half of each sardine. Close the sardines, pressing the two sides together with your fingers to seal in the filling.

Preheat the oven to 375° F. Lightly oil a baking pan and arrange the stuffed sardines in it, overlapping them with the tails on top for a decorative presentation. Place bay leaves between the sardines.

Sprinkle the sardines with the remaining bread crumbs, the sugar, and the lemon juice and bake uncovered for 20 minutes. Serve hot or at room temperature.

Sarde a Beccaficu alla Catanese

STUFFED FRIED SARDINES, CATANIA STYLE

This deep-fried version has practically nothing to do with the baked Palermitan dish that goes by the same name in Italian. The sardines are split open, marinated in vinegar, and pressed together in pairs to form "sandwiches" filled with the bread crumb-cheese mixture. Don't get discouraged if you have trouble assembling the fish "sandwiches"; they magically hold together during the frying. Serves 4. Photo opposite page 117.

Ingredients

1 pound sardines, fresh or frozen
2 cups wine vinegar
½ cup dry bread crumbs
2 tablespoons freshly grated pecorino cheese
2 beaten eggs in separate dishes
1 clove garlic
1 tablespoon parsley
Salt and black pepper
Flour for dredging
Oil for deep-frying

"Butterfly" the sardines lengthwise without separating the halves. Bone them, and marinate them in the wine vinegar for 1 hour.

Combine the bread crumbs, pecorino cheese, and 1 beaten egg. Chop the garlic and parsley together to form a homogenous mince, and add it to the bread-crumb mixture. Add salt and pepper to taste.

Drain the sardines and pat them dry. Holding one open sardine in the palm of your hand, spread it with the bread-crumb mixture. Press another split sardine against the first, open sides together, to form a "sandwich." Press the two sardines together with your fingers to seal in the filling.

Dip each sardine "sandwich" into the remaining beaten egg and dredge in flour. Pour oil into a small saucepan to a depth of 4 inches. When it is very hot, deep-fry the sardines until they are golden brown. Serve hot or at room temperature.

Tonno in Umido

TUNA IN WHITE WINE SAUCE

In Sicily, fresh tuna is extremely popular, and Trapani's tuna hunts, the *tonnare*, are a well-known tourist attraction. Serves 4

Ingredients

3 cups dry white wine
2 bay leaves
1 teaspoon dried rosemary
1 clove garlic, peeled
1¾ pounds fresh tuna
¼ cup butter
1 tablespoon olive oil
1 onion, chopped fine
4 anchovy filets, rinsed and dried
Flour for dredging
Salt and pepper to taste

Place the wine, bay leaves, rosemary, and garlic in a glass bowl and add the tuna. Marinate for 2 hours.

Heat the butter and olive oil over a low flame in a large skillet. Add the onion and anchovies, and stir with a fork until the anchovies are dissolved.

Remove the tuna from the marinade, pat dry, and dredge in flour. Pass the marinade through a sieve, reserving the liquid.

Turn up the heat under the skillet to medium, add the tuna, and sauté on both sides until golden.

Reduce the heat to low, season with salt and pepper, add ⅓ cup of the strained marinade, cover, and cook for 45 minutes, adding marinade as needed to keep the fish moist. Serve hot, sliced and with the sauce.

Verdure

Verdure

VEGETABLES AND SALADS

Italians are blessed with vegetables as sweet and delicious as they are colorful, partly because—unlike American grocery shoppers—they won't tolerate any other kind. As a result, Italian vegetables are marvelous even when cooked simply. But the recipes in this chapter are far from plain; with such glorious produce in abundance, the traditional cooks of the Mezzogiorno can let their imaginations run wild—and they do. They stuff their artichokes, drown their broccoli in wine, and roll up and stuff their eggplant slices. On hot summer days, they create fragrant salads—like the Capri Salad with tomatoes, mozzarella, and basil, or the Fennel and Olive Salad—in no time at all. Many of the recipes in this chapter can be served as side dishes (*contorni*) or, if you favor meatless meals, as main courses. There is only one hard-and-fast rule: use the freshest seasonal vegetables you can find.

Torta di Carciofi

ARTICHOKE PIE

This is a simple-to-assemble Apulian casserole, a typical torta combining potatoes and other vegetables. Since Italians use only very fresh artichokes, they can make this dish with the whole vegetable. By using the most tightly closed artichokes you can find and performing minor surgery on them, you can produce a tasty ''pie'' of your own. Serves 4

Ingredients

5 artichokes
Juice of 1 lemon
2 tablespoons fresh Italian parsley
2 cloves garlic
1 pound potatoes, sliced very thin
2 tablespoons bread crumbs
1 anchovy filet, chopped
2 tablespoons olive oil

Cut the artichokes lengthwise into quarters. Trim off the tough outer leaves, cut off the woody ends of the stems, and scrape out the chokes with a small, sharp knife. Simmer the artichoke hearts in water to cover, with the lemon juice, until they are barely tender, about 10 minutes.

Preheat the oven to 425° F. Chop the parsley and garlic together into a homogenous mince.

Spread a layer of potatoes in the bottom of an oiled casserole. Dot them with the garlic and parsley mixture. Arrange a layer of artichoke hearts on top of the potatoes. Continue to build layers in the same order until you have used up all of the vegetables.

Mash the anchovy filet into the bread crumbs with a fork. Top the casserole with bread crumbs and a sprinkling of olive oil, and bake it for one hour, until the potatoes are cooked through and the bread crumbs form a golden crust.

Carciofi con la Mozzarella

STUFFED ARTICHOKES WITH MOZZARELLA

When I was growing up, stuffed artichokes were a treat we looked forward to on holidays. Half the fun was pulling the leaves through our teeth to get a taste of artichoke flesh and a precious bit of stuffing. With the addition of mozzarella, this Neapolitan recipe is especially rich and good. Serves 4

Ingredients

4 artichokes
Juice of 1 lemon
¼ pound mozzarella cheese, diced
1 tablespoon fresh parsley, chopped
1 beaten egg
⅓ cup grated Parmesan cheese
Salt and black pepper
2 tablespoons dry bread crumbs
1 anchovy filet, chopped
¼ cup olive oil

Trim off the outer leaves of the artichokes and cut off the woody ends of the stems so that they will stand upright. In a large saucepan of water, simmer the artichokes with the lemon juice for 20 minutes or until they are tender.

In a bowl, combine the diced mozzarella cheese, parsley, egg, Parmesan cheese, and salt and pepper to taste. Mix well.

Preheat the oven to 425° F. Drain the artichokes and pat them dry. Spread the leaves out, remove chokes, and stuff the artichokes with the cheese-parsley mixture, using a teaspoon or demitasse spoon and your hands. Place the artichokes in an oiled baking pan with a few tablespoons of water.

With a fork, mix together the bread crumbs, chopped anchovy filet, and olive oil. Sprinkle the mixture over the tops of the artichokes. Baked, uncovered, for 20 minutes.

Broccoli Affucati

DROWNED BROCCOLI

In this Sicilian recipe the broccoli is "drowned" in red wine—a noble sacrifice to your taste buds. Serve it as a *contorno,* or vegetable side dish, or as a sauce for short pasta such as penne or ziti. Serves 4

Ingredients

2 scallions, chopped
2 tablespoons chopped, fresh Italian parsley
2 pounds broccoli florets
2 tablespoons olive oil
½ tin anchovies, chopped
½ cup grated pecorino cheese with peppercorns
10 black olives, pitted
Salt and black pepper
3 cups dry red wine

In a large skillet, sauté the scallions, parsley, and broccoli florets briefly in the olive oil. Partway through the cooking stir in the anchovy filets, pecorino cheese, olives, and salt and pepper to taste.

When the broccoli is crisp and bright green (after about 6 minutes), pour in the red wine and continue cooking, partly covered, over medium heat until the wine evaporates. The broccoli should be slightly overcooked, limp and dark green.

Involtini di Verza con Riso

STUFFED RED CABBAGE

These Neapolitan rice-and-meat-stuffed cabbage leaves can be either an appetizer or a main course. They are delicious both plain or topped with tomato sauce. Serves 4

Ingredients

¾ cup rice
1 small head red cabbage
3 tablespoons butter
½ cup and ¼ cup grated pecorino or Parmesan cheese
1 egg, beaten
2 tablespoons chopped, fresh Italian parsley
Freshly grated nutmeg
Salt and black pepper
⅓ pound ground beef
3 slices prosciutto, chopped
1 recipe Tomato Sauce (optional, page 41)

Put the rice in a saucepan with 1½ cups water. Bring the water to a boil, cover the pan, lower the heat, and simmer the rice for 20 minutes or until it is tender.

Remove the leaves from the cabbage carefully, so as not to break them. In a large pot of boiling salted water parboil the leaves, one at a time, for a few seconds just until they wilt. Pat them dry.

Combine the cooked rice with one tablespoon of the butter, ½ cup of the grated cheese, the egg, parsley, nutmeg, and salt and pepper to taste. Mix well.

In a skillet, sauté the ground beef briefly in another tablespoon of butter, stirring until the meat loses its red color. Remove the skillet from heat and add the prosciutto.

Preheat the oven to 350° F. Combine the meat and rice mixtures. Place 1 tablespoon of the mixture on one end of each cabbage leaf. Roll the leaves up and tie them with twine.

Place the cabbage rolls in a buttered casserole and sprinkle with the remaining tablespoon of butter and the ¼ cup grated cheese. Bake the stuffed cabbage for 20 minutes or until the top crust is golden. Serve plain or topped with Tomato Sauce.

Parmigiana di Cavolfiore

BAKED CAULIFLOWER

When you prepare this Neapolitan recipe, be careful not to overcook the cauliflower in step 1. If you do, it will have turned to mush by the time it's through baking. Serves 4.

Ingredients

1 cauliflower
1 teaspoon salt
1 recipe Tomato Sauce (page 41)
½ cup freshly grated Parmesan cheese
½ pound mozzarella cheese, shredded
Salt and black pepper

Remove the leaves and stem from the cauliflower and cook it in a large pot of salted boiling water until it is barely tender but still very crisp, about 8 minutes.

Preheat the oven to 375° F. Cut the cauliflower into large pieces. Place them in a bowl and add half of the Tomato Sauce and all but 2 tablespoons of the Parmesan cheese. Season to taste with salt and pepper, and stir to mix.

Place half of the cauliflower mixture in an oiled casserole and cover it with half of the shredded mozzarella cheese. Add the remaining cauliflower, Parmesan cheese, and Tomato Sauce, and top with the rest of the shredded mozzarella cheese. Bake the mixture for 15 minutes, or until the mozzarella is melted and bubbly.

Parmigiana di Milinciani

EGGPLANT PARMIGIANA

If you think of this popular dish as heavy and oily, this Sicilian meatless version will come as a pleasant surprise. It can be served either as a side dish or as a main dish. Serves 4

Ingredients

1 pound eggplant
Salt
¼ cup olive oil
½ pound fresh mozzarella cheese
1 cup grated pecorino cheese
1 recipe Tomato Sauce (page 41)
2 tablespoons chopped fresh basil

Cut the eggplant into ¼-inch-thick slices. Salt the slices and weigh them down with a heavy plate or a cast-iron pot cover and let them stand for 1 hour or overnight. Drain the slices and pat them dry. In a heavy skillet, sauté the eggplant slices in the olive oil until they are golden brown on both sides. Drain them on paper towels.

Preheat the oven to 350° F. Place a layer of eggplant in a round casserole and sprinkle it with about a quarter of the mozzarella cheese, grated pecorino cheese, and Tomato Sauce. Continue to build layers until you have used up all of the ingredients. The top layer should consist of eggplant, sauce, grated pecorino cheese, and a sprinkling of basil.

Bake the eggplant for 20 minutes until the top is golden brown and bubbly.

◀ *Stuffed Fried Sardines, Catania Style*
(recipe on page 107).

Involtini di Melanzane

STUFFED EGGPLANT ROLLS

T his Sicilian dish makes a wonderful meat-less main course. Slices of eggplant are stuffed with a mixture of cheeses, eggs, bread crumbs, and tomato sauce. Serves 4

Ingredients

2 large eggplants
Salt
1/4 cup plus 2 tablespoons olive oil
1 onion, sliced
1 cup dry bread crumbs
1/2 cup grated pecorino cheese with
peppercorns
1/4 pound mozzarella cheese, diced
2 hard-cooked eggs, chopped
1 recipe Tomato Sauce (page 41)

P eel the eggplant and cut it into 1/8-inch-thick slices. Salt the slices and weigh them down with a heavy plate or a cast-iron pot cover and let them stand overnight. Drain the slices and pat them dry. In a heavy skillet, sauté the eggplant slices in the 1/4 cup olive oil until they are golden on both sides. Drain them on paper towels.

In the same skillet, sauté the sliced onion in the remaining 2 tablespoons of olive oil over medium high heat until it is golden brown. Lower the heat, add the bread crumbs, and stir the mixture until it is golden. Turn off the heat, add most of the grated pecorino cheese, all of the mozzarella, and the chopped eggs to the skillet. Mix well.

Preheat the oven to 350° F. Spread each eggplant slice with 1 teaspoon of bread-crumb stuffing and 1 teaspoon of Tomato Sauce. Roll up the slices and secure them with toothpicks. Place the involtini in an oiled baking dish, sprinkle them with olive oil, and spoon any remaining stuffing over the top. Cover with grated pecorino cheese, and heat in the oven for 15 minutes.

Melanzane Ripiene

STUFFED EGGPLANT

You can vary this meatless Sicilian recipe by adding cooked ground beef, anchovy filets, or tuna. Serves 4. Photo 1 opposite page 132.

Ingredients

4 small or 2 large eggplants
4 medium-sized onions
1/2 cup olive oil
Salt and black pepper
8 peeled and chopped Italian tomatoes
1 egg
1/2 cup grated Parmesan cheese
1/4 pound mozzarella cheese, chopped
2 tablespoons chopped fresh Italian parsley
2 tablespoons chopped capers
1 1/2 dozen green olives, pitted
1 recipe Tomato Sauce (page 41)
1/2 cup dry bread crumbs
2 tablespoons olive oil

Cut the eggplants in half lengthwise and hollow them out with a sharp knife, taking care not to puncture the skins. Chop the eggplant pulp into very small pieces.

In a skillet, sauté the onion in the olive oil until it is lightly colored. Add the chopped eggplant pulp and salt and pepper to taste. Cover the skillet and cook the eggplant mixture for 3 minutes over medium heat. Add the tomatoes and stir. Set the skillet aside to cool.

Preheat the oven to 425° F. Combine the eggplant mixture with the egg, cheeses, parsley, capers, and olives. Stuff the eggplant shells with the mixture and place them in an oiled baking dish.

Pour the Tomato Sauce over the stuffed eggplant shells. Sprinkle with the bread crumbs and the 2 tablespoons olive oil.

Bake the eggplant for 15 or 20 minutes, until a crust forms on top. Serve it at room temperature.

Melanzane a Scapece

MARINATED EGGPLANT

This simple Calabrian cold vegetable dish, fragrant with mint, is perfect for summer. Try zucchini this way, too. Serves 4

Ingredients

1 1-pound eggplant
Salt
¼ cup olive oil
3 cloves garlic
2 tablespoons fresh mint leaves
2 tablespoons vinegar

Peel the eggplant and cut it into ¼-inch-thick slices. Salt the slices, weigh them down with a heavy plate or a cast-iron pot cover, and let stand 1 hour or overnight. Drain and rinse the slices and pat them dry.

Heat the oil in a large skillet and fry the eggplant slices on both sides until golden. Drain on paper towels.

Place the eggplant slices in a glass bowl, sprinkling each with garlic, mint leaves, and salt to taste, and sprinkling the entire batch with vinegar.

Let stand for 4 hours. Serve at room temperature.

Piselli con Pancetta

PEAS WITH PANCETTA OR HAM

This simple Sicilian vegetable dish is wonderful with fresh peas from the garden. Serves 4

Ingredients

2 ounces pancetta or boiled ham
3 tablespoons olive oil
1 onion, sliced thin
½ pound peas, fresh or frozen
Salt to taste

Chop the pancetta or ham into ¼-inch pieces. Heat the oil in a medium skillet over high heat, and sauté the onion. Reduce the heat to low and add the pancetta and peas.

Pour in enough water to cover the peas, cover, and cook for 20 minutes. Drain and serve hot.

Mandorlata di Peperoni

SWEET-AND-SOUR PEPPERS WITH ALMONDS

This unusual recipe—called a *mandorlata* from the Italian word for almonds, *mandorle*—comes from Basilicata. Serves 4

Ingredients

5 medium green bell peppers
½ cup raisins
2 tablespoons olive oil
¾ cup chopped almonds
1½ tablespoons sugar
¼ cup red wine vinegar
Pinch of salt

Clean, seed, and wash the peppers; cut them in strips. Let the raisins plump in a bowl of warm water to cover for 10 minutes.

Meanwhile, heat the oil in a skillet and fry the peppers over medium low heat for 10 minutes. Add the remaining ingredients and cook for 20 minutes more, stirring occasionally. Serve hot or at room temperature.

Peperonata

STEWED PEPPERS

These stewed red and green peppers can also be served hot as a sauce for pasta. Serves 4

Ingredients

1 sweet red bell pepper
1 green bell pepper
3 sweet green Italian peppers
3 tablespoons olive oil
2 medium onions, sliced
1 bay leaf
2 cloves garlic, chopped
2 cups chopped peeled tomatoes
Salt and pepper to taste

Seed and wash the peppers, and chop them into medium-sized pieces. Heat the olive oil in a large skillet and sauté the onions with the bay leaf and garlic until the onions are transparent.

Add the peppers to the skillet and cook, stirring occasionally, over medium heat for 25 minutes or until tender. Add the tomatoes and salt, and pepper, then reduce the heat to low and cook for another 10 minutes. Serve hot or cold.

Patate Arraganate

POTATO CASSEROLE WITH OREGANO

This is a simple Apulian potato casserole. The oregano makes it wonderfully fragrant and savory. Serves 4

Ingredients

2 cloves garlic, minced
3 onions, sliced thin
2 tablespoons dried oregano
2 pounds potatoes, sliced
2 tablespoons olive oil

Preheat the oven to 375° F. Stir together the minced garlic, onions, oregano, and olive oil.

Arrange the potatoes in layers in a casserole, sprinkling each layer with the spice mixture. Pour in water to cover the potatoes and bake the casserole, uncovered, for 1 hour.

Tiella de Patate e Pomodori
APULIAN POTATO-TOMATO CASSEROLE

Like the other Apulian casseroles in this chapter, this is a cousin to the traditional Tiella alla Barese (page 72). Serves 4

Ingredients

2 pounds potatoes, sliced very thin
2 cloves garlic
2 tablespoons fresh or 2 teaspoons dried basil
1 tablespoon fresh Italian parsley
1 tablespoon fresh or 1 teaspoon dried
rosemary
2 tablespoons olive oil
1½ pounds ripe tomatoes, peeled, seeded,
and chopped
2 tablespoons dry bread crumbs

Preheat the oven to 425° F. Chop the garlic, basil, parsley, and rosemary together into a homogenous mince. Combine it with the olive oil. Add the tomatoes and toss lightly to coat them with the seasonings.

Arrange the potatoes and seasoned tomatoes in alternate layers in an oiled 3-quart casserole. Add 1 cup of cold water and sprinkle the top with the bread crumbs.

Bake the casserole, uncovered, for 1 hour or until the potatoes are tender.

Pumaruoru a Gratté

STUFFED TOMATOES

This Palermitan recipe is appropriate served either as an appetizer or a side dish. It makes a lovely presentation. Serves 4. Photo 2 following page 132.

Ingredients

12 tomatoes
2 cloves garlic, minced
1 small onion, chopped
3 tablespoons olive oil
5 anchovy filets
4 tablespoons chopped fresh Italian parsley
1/3 cup capers, drained
2 cups lightly toasted bread crumbs
2 tablespoons oregano
Salt and black pepper

Choose tomatoes that are ripe but firm. Use a small, sharp knife to core the tomatoes, removing the seeds and being careful not to puncture the skin. Remove the seeds and place the tomatoes upside down on a plate to drain.

Preheat the oven to 350° F. In a small skillet, sauté the garlic and onion in the olive oil until they are lightly colored. Stir in the anchovies with a fork part way through. In a bowl, combine this mixture with the parsley, capers, bread crumbs, oregano, and salt and pepper to taste. Use a spoon to stuff the tomatoes with the mixture.

Place the stuffed tomatoes in a baking pan with 3 or 4 tablespoons of water and bake them, uncovered, for 20 minutes.

Zucca all Agrodolce

SWEET-AND-SOUR SQUASH

The Spanish brought squash to Sicily from the New World. Sicilians ridiculed their invaders by noting that the squash (whose hollow center made it a synonym for "empty head" in popular speech) came from Spain. Prepare this a day in advance and serve it at room temperature. Serves 4

Ingredients

1 pound butternut squash
5 cloves garlic
¼ cup olive oil
1 teaspoon sugar
4 tablespoons wine vinegar
Salt
Fresh mint leaves, finely chopped

Peel the butternut squash with a vegetable peeler. Cut the squash lengthwise into slices. In a large skillet, sauté the garlic in the olive oil until it is lightly colored. Add the squash slices and sauté them until they are tender. Drain them on paper towels.

Add the sugar and vinegar to the skillet, bring it to a boil, and turn off the heat immediately.

Arrange the squash in layers in a high-sided glass bowl and add salt to taste. Pour in the vinegar-sugar sauce, turning the slices to coat them, and let the squash marinate overnight in the refrigerator. Garnish squash with mint and serve it at room temperature.

Fagioli alla Menta

MARINATED WHITE BEAN SALAD WITH MINT

Here is a simple salad, refreshed with the taste of mint. Serves 4. Photo 3 following page 132.

Ingredients

*1 pound dried cannellini (Great Northern)
beans
1 clove garlic
1 stalk celery
½ cup olive oil
½ cup white wine vinegar
2 tablespoons chopped fresh mint leaves
Salt and black pepper*

Soak the beans overnight in water to cover. Simmer the beans, uncovered, in a large pot of salted water with the garlic and celery until it is tender, about 2½ hours.

Drain the beans, remove and discard the garlic and celery, and place the beans in a salad bowl with the oil, vinegar, mint, and salt and pepper to taste. Toss to mix, cover, and let stand for 1 hour in a cool place before serving.

Insalata Caprese

CAPRI SALAD

This delicious salad makes the perfect summer lunch or supper when the tomatoes in your garden are weighing down the vines. Fresh snow-white mozzarella is essential to the flavor, as are fruity, pure olive oil and fresh basil. Serves 4

Ingredients

1 pound ripe tomatoes
½ pound fresh mozzarella cheese
3 tablespoons chopped fresh basil leaves
¼ cup olive oil
Salt

Slice the tomatoes and the mozzarella cheese about ¼ inch thick.

Alternate the tomato and mozzarella slices on a platter, overlapping them. Sprinkle with the basil, olive oil, and salt to taste.

Insalata de Finocchio ed Olive

FENNEL AND OLIVE SALAD

The crisp anise and the strong olive taste are wonderful counterpoints to each other. Serves 4. Photo 4 following page 132.

Ingredients

1 medium head Florence fennel (anise)
12 green olives, pitted
1 tablespoon chopped fresh Italian parsley
3 tablespoons fruity olive oil
1 tablespoon wine vinegar
1 clove garlic, minced
1 teaspoon oregano
Black pepper to taste

Remove the top from the fennel and cut the bulb into chunks. Combine the fennel chunks, olives, and parsley in a salad bowl.

With a fork, stir together the oil, vinegar, minced garlic, oregano, and pepper, and pour the dressing over the salad. Toss well and serve.

Insalata di Arance

ORANGE SALAD

With the abundance of citrus fruit in Sicily, it's not surprising that oranges even find their way into salads. This is a refreshing and unusual summer accompaniment to chicken, beef, or fish. Don't add olives until you're ready to serve the dish; they will leave blotches on the oranges. Serves 4

Ingredients

4 medium-sized oranges
1 tablespoon olive oil
1 tablespoon wine vinegar
Salt and black pepper
¹/₃ cup green olives, pitted and chopped
(optional)

Peel the oranges and remove all of the bitter white membrane. Separate the sections and cut them in half if they are large.

Immediately before serving, combine the oil, vinegar, and salt and pepper to taste. Add the olives to the orange sections if desired and sprinkle the oil-vinegar dressing over them.

Opposite: Stuffed Eggplant ▶
(recipe on page 119).
Following page: Stuffed Tomatoes
(recipe on page 126).

Dolci

◀ *Opposite: Fennel and Olive Salad*
(recipe on page 130).
Preceding page: Marinated White Bean
Salad with Mint (recipe on page 128).

133

Dolci

DESSERTS AND PASTRIES

Like all Italians, southerners like to conclude their meals with fresh fruit—sweet, juicy peaches, pears, and oranges, luscious red watermelon wedges. But when they unleash their imaginations on desserts and pastries, the results clearly rank as Italy's best. The variety—most notably in Sicily—is dazzling, from the traditional cannoli and cassata, enjoyed in pastry shops on both sides of the Atlantic, to modern creations like Coccoddè, zabaglione ice cream with whipped cream arranged to look like a plate of fried eggs. Here southern culinary whimsy is very much in evidence, from the "pizza" made with strawberries and pastry cream to Minni di Vergini, "breasts of the Virgin," traditionally made in convents and topped with soft white meringue. I've included many old favorites you may have sampled at your grandmother's home or, with a cup of espresso at an Italian café. Other recipes are less familiar but equally enticing, such as the traditional Neapolitan Easter cake, Pastiera. For the busy cook, there are also easy treats, like the refreshing ices called Granite. You may find, as southern Italians themselves do, that these pastries are too rich to be appreciated after a meal. If so, why not serve them when you have guests over for coffee—preferably espresso?

Gelu i Muluni

WATERMELON "PUDDING"

This unusual dessert is a Sicilian favorite full of the tastes of summer and the island's Arab conquerors—watermelon, pistachios, and cinnamon. You can make this dessert in individual molds. Serves 4

Ingredients

2 pounds watermelon pulp, cut into chunks
2 cups sugar
6 tablespoons cornstarch
1 teaspoon rose water or vanilla extract
Pinch of cinnamon
⅓ cup candied fruit, chopped
⅓ cup semisweet chocolate, finely chopped
1 tablespoon undyed pistachios, shelled and chopped

Force the melon through a sieve twice. In a saucepan, stir the sugar into the melon juice. Over a low flame, stir in the cornstarch, mixing well to dissolve it. Add the rose water or vanilla and the cinnamon, turn the heat up to medium and continue cooking, stirring constantly until the mixture is thick and glossy.

Remove the pan from the heat, cool to lukewarm, and stir in the candied fruit and chocolate. Pour the mixture into a wet 1½-quart mold. Chill in the refrigerator for 3 hours or overnight. Unmold and serve garnished with chopped pistachios.

Coccoddè

ZABAGLIONE ICE CREAM "FRIED EGGS"

This spectacular ice-cream dish, with its scoops of honey-coated zabaglione ice cream surrounded by whipped cream sprinkled with cinnamon, looks just like a plate of fried eggs, complete with scorched edges. I first enjoyed it at an outdoor ice cream café in the main square of Acireale (near Taormina), a town with lovely baroque wedding-cake architecture. You will need an ice-cream machine, either hand-cranked or electric. Serves 4

Ingredients

6 egg yolks
¾ cup sugar
Salt
1 cup milk
4 cups heavy cream
1 tablespoon vanilla extract
½ cup dry Marsala
¼ cup honey
Dash of cinnamon

In the top of a double boiler over hot water, combine 3 egg yolks, ½ cup of the sugar, and salt to taste, stirring with a whisk. In a saucepan, heat the milk. Stir it gradually into the egg mixture over medium heat until the mixture thickens. Let it cool.

When the mixture is cool, stir in 2 cups of heavy cream and vanilla, and process in an ice-cream maker according to manufacturer's directions. Set aside.

Meanwhile, to make the zabaglione, combine the remaining 3 egg yolks, the ¼ cup sugar, and the Marsala in top of a double boiler over hot water. Beat with a wire whisk until the mixture forms a dense foam. Let it cool, fold it into the soft ice cream with a rubber spatula, and place the ice cream in the freezer compartment of your refrigerator to "ripen," or harden.

Assemble the dessert. Whip the remaining 2 cups cream. Place 2 or 3 scoops of ice cream on each serving plate. Spoon honey over each scoop. Use a rubber spatula to arrange the whipped cream around the "yolks" to form the "whites." Sprinkle cinnamon to simulate scorched edges. Serve immediately.

Granita di Limone

LEMON ICE

This popular Sicilian summer refreshment, just the thing for cooling off as you relax in a Taormina square late in the evening, is popular all over Italy. Fresh lemon juice is essential to the taste of the ice. I offer two alternate methods—one for the orthodox, the other for the busy cook. Serves 4. Photo 4 following page 148.

Ingredients

1 cup freshly squeezed lemon juice
2 cups water
½ cup sugar
Rind of 1 lemon, grated

Combine all of the ingredients in a saucepan over low heat, stirring until the sugar has dissolved and the mixture is transparent.

The orthodox method calls for placing the mixture in the freezer for 3 hours and stirring with a fork every 30 minutes to break up the ice crystals. The easy way allows you to freeze the mixture for 3 hours and break up the crystals only once, immediately before serving, in a blender or food processor. The first method produces an ice of far finer texture, and the best Sicilian cooks prefer it.

Granita di Caffe

COFFEE ICE

This ice co-stars with the preceding granita as Sicily's favorite. It's important to use high-quality espresso coffee, preferably freshly ground. Be careful not to eat too much of this ice at one sitting, no matter how refreshing, or you will be climbing the walls from a caffeine overdose. Serves 4

Ingredients

1½ cups strong freshly brewed espresso coffee
¾ cup milk
¼ cup sugar

Combine all of the ingredients in a saucepan over low heat, stirring until the sugar has dissolved.

The orthodox method calls for placing the mixture in the freezer for 3 hours and stirring with a fork every 30 minutes to break up the ice crystals. The easy way allows you to freeze the mixture for 3 hours and break up the crystals only once, immediately before serving, in a blender or food processor. The first method produces an ice of far finer texture.

Pizza di Crema e Fragole

PASTRY CREAM AND STRAWBERRY PIZZA

This is a sweet version of the popular *pizza rustica,* or covered pizza, in which the pastry cream and strawberries look like ricotta and prosciutto. Serves 4. Photo 1 opposite page 148.

Pastry

2 cups flour
½ cup sugar
¼ pound butter (1 stick)
2 tablespoons lard
2 large eggs
Rind of 1 lemon or orange, grated

Sift together the flour and sugar and cut in the butter and lard with a pastry cutter. Stir in the eggs and rind and knead the mixture briefly to form a soft but not sticky dough. (If you use a food processor, first combine the flour and sugar in the work bowl. Turn the machine on and off. Add the butter and lard and process the mixture until it resembles cornmeal. Add the eggs and rind and process until the dough forms a ball.)

Wrap the dough in plastic wrap and chill it for half an hour in the refrigerator while you prepare the filling.

Filling

1 pound strawberries
13 tablespoons (¾ cup + 1 tablespoon sugar)
6 egg yolks
6 tablespoons all-purpose flour
2 cups milk

Combine the strawberries with 6 tablespoons sugar and refrigerate.

Mix together the remaining 7 tablespoons sugar, egg yolks, and flour in the top of a double boiler over hot water. Heat the milk in a saucepan and stir it gradually into the mixture in the double boiler. Continue heating for 10 minutes or until the mixture thickens. Cool.

Assembly

{ {

4 tablespoons confectioner's sugar

Preheat the oven to 400° F. Roll out two thirds of the dough and fit it into a buttered 9½-inch springform pan. Spread the filling over the bottom. Top with the strawberries. Roll the remaining dough into a thin sheet and lay it over the top of the pie.

Bake for 40 minutes or until the crust is golden. When the pie is cool, sprinkle it with confectioner's sugar.

Cassata Siciliana

Athough many variations of this recipe have circulated in the United States, including the frozen version that is also popular in Italy, this is the original: a simple, sweetened ricotta, with nuts and candied fruits, encased in sponge cake. Sicilian pastry chefs turn it into a baroque extravaganza with elaborate icings decorated with candied fruit slivers. Busy cooks might wish to dust the cake with confectioner's sugar instead. Serves 8. Photo 2 following page 148.

Cake

5 large eggs, separated
½ teaspoon salt
1½ cups sugar
Rind of 1 lemon, grated
1⅛ cups flour
½ teaspoon cream of tartar

Butter and flour 2 eight-inch round cake pans. Preheat the oven to 350°F.

Beat the egg whites until they are stiff but not dry, folding in the salt and ½ cup of the sugar part way through.

Beat the egg yolks with the remaining 1 cup sugar and lemon rind. Fold the yolks into the whites with a rubber spatula.

Sift the flour with the cream of tartar twice, and fold it into the eggs. Pour the mixture into the cake pans. Bake the cakes for 40 minutes, until the tops are golden. Let cool.

Filling

2 pounds part-skim ricotta
2 cups confectioner's sugar
2 teaspoons cinnamon
¼ cup semisweet chocolate pieces
¼ cup chopped candied fruit
½ cup chopped pistachios or pine nuts

Force the ricotta through a sieve. Combine with the remaining ingredients and set aside.

Assembly

6 tablespoons liqueur or Marsala
Confectioner's sugar

Assemble the cake. Cut cake into strips or slices and sprinkle with liqueur or Marsala. Line the sides, bottom, and top of a 10-cup round mold with strips of cake. Fill the mold with the creamy ricotta. Top with a layer of cake, pressing it down to fill the mold solidly. Cover with plastic wrap and chill for 4 to 6 hours.

Unmold the cake and sprinkle it with confectioner's sugar before serving.

Cannoli

These ricotta-cream-filled pastry shells are one of the most glorious legacies of Arab-Sicilian cuisine. A tradition at Carnival time, they have earned year-round popularity on both sides of the Atlantic. To make the shells, you will need metal cannoli forms, or you can use the sawed-off end of a broom handle according to custom! If you're in a rush, you can purchase the shells at a bakery and stuff them with homemade filling just before serving. Serves 4. Photo 3 following page 148.

Shells

1½ cups flour
1 tablespoon sugar
Pinch of salt
1½ teaspoons unsweetened cocoa
1½ teaspoons instant coffee powder
1 tablespoon lard or vegetable shortening
½ cup dry-red wine or dry Marsala
1 egg white
Sunflower oil for deep-frying

Sift together the flour, sugar, salt, cocoa, and coffee powder. Cut in the lard with a pastry blender or in the food processor. Then work the wine in gradually, kneading with your hands to make a soft dough.

Roll the dough out on a lightly floured surface. Using a 5-inch round cutter (a bowl will do), cut 12 discs.

Wrap the discs around the oiled cannoli forms, sealing the edges with the egg white.

Pour oil into a small saucepan to a depth of about 4 inches. When it is very hot, deep-fry the shells one at a time until they are golden and crisp, about 4 seconds. As you retrieve the shells with a slotted spoon, be careful to tip each one so that any oil inside the cylinder is poured back into the pan instead of on your hand. Drain the shells on paper towels and carefully slip the metal forms out when they're cool enough to handle. Continue this procedure with the remaining pastry discs.

Filling

½ pound part-skim ricotta
1¼ cups confectioner's sugar
2 tablespoons candied fruit
¼ cup chocolate chips
⅓ teaspoon ground cinnamon
¼ cup finely chopped undyed pistachios

Press the ricotta and sugar through a sieve and stir in the remaining ingredients. Blend well.

Assembly

12 candied cherries (not maraschino)
12 pieces candied orange rind

Stuff the cannoli shells carefully with ricotta cream, using a demitasse spoon. It is extremely important that you wait until serving time to stuff the cannoli, or the shells will become soggy.

Place 1 cherry and 1 piece of candied orange rind on the filling at either end of each pastry.

Zeppole

These simple fritters are popular throughout the Italian South. Garnished with pastry cream, they are traditional for Saint Joseph's Day. This is the plain version, sprinkled with confectioner's sugar. Serves 4

Ingredients

2 cups water
½ cup cognac
1 tablespoon sugar
Pinch of salt
2 cups all-purpose flour
Sunflower oil for deep-frying
½ cup confectioner's sugar

Combine the water, cognac, sugar, and salt, and bring to a boil in a heavy saucepan over medium high heat.

Remove from heat and stir in the flour all at once. Over a medium flame, continue mixing until the dough pulls away from the sides of the pan.

Turn out the dough onto an oiled surface. Knead it with a rolling pin for 10 minutes, continually folding it over and rolling it out. Use your hands to mold it into a long roll about ½ inch in diameter. Cut it into segments 6 inches long and curl each segment into a doughnut-shaped ring.

Pierce the rings well with a fork to prevent them from erupting as dangerously as Vesuvius during the deep-frying. Pour oil into a saucepan to a depth of about 4 inches. When it is very hot, deep-fry the zeppole two or three at a time until they are deep gold, about 5 minutes. Sprinkle them with confectioner's sugar and serve hot.

Crispelle di Riso alla Benedettina

These cinnamon-flavored rice croquettes, coated with honey, are a very unusual Sicilian dessert. Serves 6 to 8

Ingredients

1 cup rice
2 cups milk
1 envelope active dry yeast
Rind of 1 lemon, grated
3 tablespoons flour
Pinch of salt
Flour for dredging
⅛ cup sugar
½ teaspoon ground cinnamon
Sunflower oil for deep-frying
⅓ cup honey

In a saucepan, cook the rice and milk together over medium heat. When the milk reaches a boil, lower the heat, cover the pan, and simmer the rice gently until it has absorbed the milk; it will still be creamy. Remove the pan from heat and cool slightly.

Dissolve the yeast in ¼ cup warm water and stir it into the rice. Stir in the lemon rind, flour, and salt, and let the mixture stand for 1 hour.

Mold the flavored rice into cylinders about 2½ inches long. Dredge the cylinders in the additional flour.

Combine the sugar and cinnamon. Pour oil into a small saucepan to a depth of about 4 inches. When it is very hot, deep-fry the croquettes until they are golden. Roll them in the cinnamon sugar and sprinkle them with honey. Serve at once.

Taralli

These simple iced cookies are familiar to many Americans of southern Italian descent. Boiling them briefly before baking gives them a shiny exterior. Yields 3 dozen

Ingredients

2²/₃ cups all-purpose flour
¼ cup sugar
4 to 6 tablespoons dry white wine
Pinch of salt
1 teaspoon sunflower oil
1 cup sugar
2 tablespoons water
Pinch of ground cinnamon

Combine the flour, sugar, 4 tablespoons of the wine, salt, and oil, and mix well to form a smooth dough. If necessary to soften the dough, add 1 or 2 more tablespoons of wine. Shape the dough into sausage-like rolls about 4 inches long and curl them into doughnut-shaped rings.

Preheat the oven to 350° F. Drop the rings into a 3-quart saucepan of boiling water a few at a time and cook them for several seconds. When they rise to the top, retrieve them with a slotted spoon and drain them on paper towels. Place them on a baking sheet. Bake the taralli for 1 hour and 10 minutes.

Melt the sugar and water together in a saucepan over low heat, stirring until the sugar dissolves. Remove the saucepan from the heat, stir in the cinnamon, and beat the mixture with an electric mixer at medium speed just until thick. Spread the icing over the taralli with a knife or the back of a spoon.

Opposite: Pastry Cream and Strawberry Pizza ▶
(recipe on page 140).
Following page: Cassata Siciliana
(recipe on page 142).

Chiacchiere

These fried strips of dough sprinkled with confectioner's sugar are known by many different names; this one comes from the verb "to chat," and indeed they're perfect with coffee and conversation. Yields 3 dozen.

Ingredients

3 eggs
4 tablespoons unsalted butter, softened
2 cups unbleached all-purpose flour
Pinch of salt
Sunflower oil for deep-frying
¾ cup confectioner's sugar

With an electric mixer, combine the eggs, butter, flour, and salt. Cover the dough with a damp towel and let it rest for 30 minutes.

On a floured surface, roll the dough out into a translucent sheet about ⅛ inch thick. With a fluted ravioli wheel, cut the sheet into strips about 1 inch wide.

Pour oil into a medium-sized saucepan to a depth of about 4 inches. When it is very hot, deep-fry the chiacchiere a few at a time until they are puffed and golden. Drain them on paper towels, sprinkle them with confectioner's sugar, and serve them warm.

◀ *Opposite: Lemon Ice (recipe on page 138)*
and Chiacchiere.
Preceding page: Cannoli (recipe on page 144).   149

Pignolata alla Messinese

These small, deep-fried cookies are piled high on a plate to resemble a mountain and coated with white and chocolate icing, a construction somewhat similar to croquembouche. They are Messina's most famous pastry, and they are on display in every bakery window. Yields 3 dozen

Ingredients

4 cups unbleached all-purpose flour
1/4 pound butter (1 stick)
5 large eggs
Pinch of salt
Sunflower oil for deep-frying
8 ounces semisweet chocolate
3 1/2 cups sugar
1 egg white
Rind of 1 lemon, grated
2 tablespoons chopped candied fruit

With an electric mixer, combine the flour, butter, 5 eggs, and salt into a dough that is smooth and elastic. Cover the dough and let it rest for 30 minutes.

Mold the dough into a long sausage-like cylinder and cut it into 1-inch segments. Pour oil into a small saucepan to a depth of about 4 inches. When it is very hot, deep-fry the segments a few at a time until they are golden. Drain them on paper towels.

Melt the chocolate in a saucepan over very low heat or in the top of a double boiler over hot water. Stir in the 1/2 cup sugar and mix well. Set aside.

With an electric mixer, combine the remaining 3 cups sugar, the egg white, lemon peel, and candied fruit. You will now have two icings, one chocolate and one white.

Pile the cookies on a plate to form a mountain. Using a spatula, pour the white icing over half of the mound. Then cover the other half with the chocolate icing.

Struffoli

These popular and colorful Neapolitan Christmas cookies are always a hit—especially when they are homemade. They are actually very easy to prepare. The dough is identical to that used for Pignolata alla Messinese. Yields 3 dozen

Ingredients

4 cups unbleached all-purpose flour
¼ pound (1 stick) butter, softened
5 large eggs
Pinch of salt
Sunflower oil for deep-frying
½ cup honey
1 tablespoon sugar
2 tablespoons water
¾ cup chopped candied fruit

With an electric mixer, combine the flour, butter, 5 eggs, and salt into a dough that is smooth and elastic. Cover the dough and let it rest for 30 minutes.

Mold the dough into tiny balls, each about ½ inch in diameter.

Pour oil into a small saucepan to a depth of about 4 inches. When it is very hot, deep-fry the balls a few at a time until they are golden. Drain them on paper towels.

In a large saucepan, slowly heat the honey, sugar, and water until the mixture is golden-brown and smooth. Drop the struffoli into the honey, stir, and pour the mixture out on a plate. Shape it into a mound and sprinkle it with candied fruit.

Minni di Vergini

BREASTS OF THE VIRGIN

These look exactly like what they are supposed to, and are a traditional Sicilian convent specialty, along with the cookies named after the breasts of the martyred St. Agatha. There's a funny scene in Lampedusa's famous novel of Sicilian upper-class life, *The Leopard,* in which the hero, Don Fabrizio, wonders about the cookies as he takes some on his dessert plate. "Why ever didn't the Holy Office forbid these cakes when it had the chance?" he asks. Not all versions contain pastry cream. Yields 3 dozen. Photo opposite page 164.

Pastry

2²/₃ cups unbleached all-purpose flour
²/₃ cup sugar
²/₃ cup lard
1 egg
¹/₄ cup milk

Using an electric mixer, food processor, or pastry cutter, combine the flour, sugar, lard, and egg. Add milk as needed to make a soft dough; you may not need to use all of the milk. Chill the dough for 30 minutes.

Pastry Cream

6 eggs, separated
³/₄ cup sugar
¹/₂ cup cornstarch
4 cups milk
Rind of 1 lemon, grated
1 teaspoon vanilla extract
Pinch of ground cinnamon

Prepare the pastry cream. With a wire whisk, beat together the egg yolks and sugar. In the top of a double boiler, stir the cornstarch into the milk until it is suspended. Add the lemon rind, vanilla extract, and cinnamon. Heat the mixture over very hot water, stirring continuously, until it thickens. Set the pastry cream aside to cool.

Assembly

4 tablespoons chocolate chips
4 tablespoons chopped candied fruit
1 egg white and 5 egg whites in separate
dishes
Confectioner's sugar

On a floured surface, roll out half of the dough. Stir the chocolate chips and candied fruit into the pastry cream. Drop heaping tablespoonfuls of the pastry cream in rows on the dough, spacing the gobs of cream about ½ inch apart. Brush the spaces with the 1 egg white. Roll out the remaining half of the dough and lay it carefully on top of the layer dotted with filling, pressing down between the lumps to seal the filling in. Cut the cookies in rounds, each containing filling.

Preheat the oven to 375° F. Beat the remaining 5 egg whites until they are stiff but not dry. Spread the beaten egg whites over the tops of the cookies so that they are smooth white mounds. Transfer the cookies to a baking sheet and bake them for 45 minutes, sprinkling with confectioner's sugar just before they come out of the oven.

Ravioli Dolci di Carnevale

SWEET CARNIVAL RAVIOLI

These ravioli have a sweet dough. They are filled with sweetened ricotta and deep-fried until crisp. Yields 3 dozen

Dough

2½ cups unbleached all-purpose flour
3 large eggs
¼ cup sugar
¼ teaspoon vanilla extract

Place the flour in a mound on a pastry board. Make a well in the center. Place the eggs, sugar, and vanilla in the well and stir with a fork into the flour, incorporating the flour gradually into the wet mixture. Use your hands to knead until it becomes a soft pastry dough. Chill the dough for 30 minutes.

Filling

1¾ cups part-skim ricotta
½ cup sugar
Pinch of ground cinnamon
Rind of ½ lemon, grated
4 tablespoons grated orange rind

Force the ricotta through a sieve. Stir the sugar, cinnamon, lemon rind, and orange rind into the ricotta and set the mixture aside.

Assembly

Sunflower oil for deep-frying
Confectioner's sugar

On a lightly floured surface, roll half of the dough out into a thin sheet. Using half of the filling, drop tablespoons of filling about ½ inch apart on half of the sheet of dough. Fold over the other half of the dough and press the edges together to seal in the filling. Use a pastry wheel to cut the ravioli into pockets about 1½ inches square. Repeat this procedure with the remaining dough and filling.

Pour oil into a small saucepan to a depth of about 4 inches. When it is very hot, deep-fry the ravioli a few at a time until they are golden. Drain them on paper towels and dust them with confectioner's sugar before serving.

Pastiera

This is the traditional Easter cake of Naples. The grain symbolizes the fertility of spring. Serves 4 to 6

Ingredients

2 cups unbleached all-purpose flour
1/2 cup sugar
1/4 pound butter (1 stick)
2 tablespoons lard
2 large eggs
Rind of 1 lemon or orange, grated

Sift together the flour and sugar and cut in the butter and lard with a pastry cutter. Stir in the eggs and grated rind and knead the mixture briefly to form a soft but not sticky dough. If you use a food processor, combine the flour and sugar in the work bowl. Turn the machine on and off. Add the butter and lard and process the mixture until it resembles cornmeal. Add the eggs and rind and process the dough until it forms a ball. Chill the dough for 30 minutes.

Filling

5 eggs, separated
1 1/3 cups milk
1 1/4 cups + 2 tablespoons sugar
1 tablespoon cornstarch
1/2 teaspoon vanilla extract
1 pound part-skim ricotta
1 tablespoon orange flower water
1 2/3 cups packaged bulgur wheat, cooked
according to package directions
1/3 cup chopped candied fruit
1 tablespoon unsalted butter, cut up
Confectioner's sugar

Prepare the pastry cream: Using a wire whisk, combine 2 of the egg yolks, the milk, the 2 tablespoons sugar, the cornstarch, and vanilla extract. Heat the mixture in the top of a double boiler over very hot water, stirring continuously with a wooden spoon, until it thickens. Set the pastry cream aside to cool.

Force the ricotta through a sieve. Stir the remaining 1¼ cups sugar, 3 egg yolks, orange flower water, cooked wheat, and the candied fruit into the ricotta and fold in the cooled pastry cream. Beat all of the egg whites until they are stiff but not dry. Fold the egg whites into the ricotta mixture.

On a lightly floured surface, roll out two thirds of the dough into a circle. Fold it carefully in quarters and transfer it to a well-buttered 9½-inch springform pan. Unfold the dough and arrange it carefully to form a bottom crust. Pour in the ricotta filling and dot the top of it with butter.

Preheat the oven to 350° F. Roll out the remaining dough and cut it into strips with a pastry wheel. Crisscross the strips on top of the filled pastry to form a lattice. Bake the pastiera for 2 hours. Dust the top with confectioner's sugar and let stand for 2 hours before removing the sides of the pan. Wait 24 hours before serving.

Crostata di Ricotta

ITALIAN CHEESECAKE

By beating the egg whites well and baking only as long as necessary, you can be sure your cheesecake will be light and not at all dry. Serves 4 to 6

Ingredients

2 cups unbleached all-purpose flour
1/2 cup sugar
1/4 pound butter (1 stick)
2 tablespoons lard
2 large eggs
Rind of 1 lemon or orange, grated
1 egg yolk (reserved from filling)

Sift together the flour and sugar and cut in the butter and lard with a pastry cutter. Stir in the eggs and grated rind and knead the mixture briefly to form a soft but not sticky dough. If you use a food processor, combine the flour and sugar in the work bowl. Turn the machine on and off. Add the butter and lard and process the mixture until it resembles cornmeal. Add the eggs and rind and process the dough until it forms a ball. Chill the dough for 30 minutes.

Filling

3 cups part-skim ricotta
3/4 cup sugar
1/2 cup chopped candied fruit
1/2 cup chocolate chips
4 eggs, separated

Force the ricotta for the filling through a sieve. Stir the sugar, candied fruit, chocolate chips, and 3 of the egg yolks into the ricotta. (Reserve the fourth egg yolk.)

Beat the egg whites until they are stiff but not dry, and fold them into the ricotta mixture.

On a lightly floured surface, roll out two thirds of the dough. Fold it carefully in quarters and transfer it to a well-buttered 9½-inch springform pan. Unfold the dough and arrange it carefully to form a bottom crust. Pour in the ricotta filling.

Preheat the oven to 425° F. Roll out the remaining dough into a circle and place it on top of the filling, pressing the edges of the crusts to seal them together. Brush the top crust with egg yolk. Bake the cheesecake for 40 minutes. Do not remove the sides of the pan until the cheesecake has completely cooled.

Fichi Farciti

STUFFED FIGS

This Calabrian recipe is a healthful snack for kids, an alternative to sugar candy. Yields 3 dozen. Photo opposite page 165.

Ingredients

½ cup almonds
1 teaspoon ground cinnamon
3 tablespoons chopped candied fruit
2 cups dried figs
2 ounces unsweetened chocolate

Preheat the oven to 250° F. and toast the almonds for 5 minutes or until they are golden. Turn the oven up to 350° F. Chop the almonds very finely and combine them with the cinnamon and candied fruit.

Cut the figs in half lengthwise and stuff them with the almond mixture, pressing them tightly closed with your hand to seal in the filling.

Melt the chocolate in the top of a double boiler over hot water. Bake the figs for 7 minutes or until they are lightly browned. Brush them with melted chocolate and serve them hot.

Cubbaita di Giuggiulena

SESAME-ALMOND TORRONE

This wonderful Sicilian nougat is nothing like the traditional torrone of Cremona more widely sold in the United States at Christmastime. An Arabic legacy, as reflected in its name, cubbaita, it is extremely decorative and simple to make. Serves 4 to 6

Ingredients

1 pound almonds, chopped
2²/₃ cups sugar
1 cup sesame seeds
½ cup honey

Preheat the oven to 250° F. and toast the almonds for 5 minutes or until they are golden. Let cool.

In a heavy saucepan, cook the sugar slowly until it melts. Stir in the sesame seeds, almonds, and honey and cook the mixture for a minute or two over low heat until the honey dissolves.

Turn the mixture out onto a large plate and use a wet knife to mold it into a large rectangular cake no more than 1 inch high. When the cake has cooled to lukewarm cut it into slices with an oiled knife. Serve cool.

Zuppa Inglese

"ENGLISH SOUP"

There is a great deal of controversy over the origin of the name of this rich dessert, but many maintain it is an Italian variation of English trifle. Some versions incorporate an egg custard, like the Neapolitan one below; others feature ricotta. It should be prepared a day in advance. Serves 4 to 6

Cake

5 large eggs, separated
½ teaspoon salt
1½ cups sugar
Rind of 1 lemon, grated
1⅛ cups flour
½ teaspoon cream of tartar

Butter and flour 2 eight-inch round cake pans. Preheat the oven to 350° F.

Beat the egg whites until they are stiff but not dry, folding in the salt and ½ cup sugar part way through. Beat the egg yolks with 1 cup sugar and the lemon rind. Fold the yolks into the whites with a rubber spatula.

Sift the flour with the cream of tartar twice, and fold it into the eggs. Pour the mixture into the cake pans. Bake the cakes for 40 minutes, until the tops are golden.

Custard

6 egg yolks, beaten
6 tablespoons sugar
4 cups milk
2 tablespoons cornstarch

Beat the egg yolks and sugar together well. Add the milk, stir well, and place in the top part of a double boiler over very hot water. When the mixture is hot, pour ½ cup of it into the cornstarch and stir into the rest of the custard. Cook for 20 minutes, until the custard has thickened (it will still be fairly liquid).

Assembly

½ cup rum
6 tablespoons sugar
1 pint strawberries
6 egg whites

Cut the sponge layers into quarters and place them in a 3-quart ovenproof casserole. Sprinkle with the rum and pour the custard over the cake.

Stir 2 tablespoons of sugar into the strawberries and scatter them over the custard and cake.

Beat the egg whites until they are stiff, adding 3 tablespoons of sugar part way through. Spread the meringue over the top of the zuppa inglese in peaks, making it higher in the center. Sprinkle remaining 1 tablespoon of sugar over the meringue and bake at 250° F. for 20 minutes, until the top is lightly golden. Place in the refrigerator overnight and serve cold.

"Breasts of the Virgin" pastries ▶
(recipe on pages 152-153).

Menus

Menus

You will get the most enjoyment from this book if you take full advantage of the versatility of southern Italian cooking. To some extent, that means taking the chapter divisions with a grain of salt. Although some people prefer to stand by the traditional Italian menu—appetizer, first course, second course with *contorno*, fruit for dessert—there is no law that says you can't assemble a wonderful meal with one of the recipes in the Vegetables chapter, such as Stuffed Red Cabbage or Stuffed Eggplant Rolls, and a salad; then you can let go with a rich dessert such as Italian Cheesecake. There are historic precedents for this. As I have mentioned, antipasti and what we think of as side dishes were often the only thing a peasant had for dinner. And dishes such as Swordfish Pie were originally *piatti unici* that render the pasta course superfluous. The following menus are intended as guidelines to show how traditional southern Italian recipes work at the contemporary American dinner table.

Brunch

Eggs in Purgatory
Garlic bread*
Pastry Cream and Strawberry Pizza

Winter Lunch

Thousand Little Things Soup
Stuffed Calzone
Fresh apples and bananas*

Spring Lunch

Sicilian Frittata
Tossed salad*
Taralli

Summer Lunch

Pizza Margherita
Green salad*
Watermelon ''Pudding''

Vegetarian Dinner

Mozzarella in Carozza
Stuffed Eggplant
Fennel and Olive Salad
Zabaglione Ice Cream ''Fried Eggs''

Winter Dinner

Ripiddu Nivicatu
Steak with Vinegar
Marinated White Bean Salad with Mint
Green salad*
Cannoli

Summer Dinner

Bucatini, Cart Driver's Style
Sweet-and-Sour Stuffed Grilled Swordfish
Green salad*
Watermelon wedges*

*Recipe not in book.

Christmas Eve Dinner

Eggplant Caponata
Pasta Palina
Fried Salt Cod
Zuppa di Pesce
Stuffed Artichokes with Mozzarella
Cassata
Struffoli

Easter Dinner

Sicilian Sweet-and-Sour Vegetables
Spaghetti with Fried Zucchini
Lamb Hunter's Style or roast lamb* with
Stuffed Tomatoes
Pastiera

Techniques

Techniques

MAKING PASTA

There are several ways to make pasta—by hand, in a food processor, or in a hand-cranked pasta machine. Electric pasta machines are also available, but they are expensive, and, since each one comes with its own instruction manual, we won't discuss them here.

If you want to make pasta by hand, you would be wise to read the directions that follow. Study them carefully several times before you crack your first egg. If you have to pore over instructions after you start to work, the dough will dry out and become difficult or even impossible to work with.

Although there is nothing like well-made hand-kneaded pasta, the food processor also produces good results, and if you own one you will surely want to put it to use.

The hand-cranked pasta machine is probably the best all-round pasta maker—unless you have an expert grandmother to do it for you. The machine makes fine sheets of pasta; it is easy to clean and inexpensive as well. You will have great versatility if you choose a machine with interchangeable rollers. If you own both a hand-cranked pasta machine and a food processor, you will probably learn for yourself that the two machines can be put to work as a team. The combination is almost as convenient as an expensive electric pasta maker.

In the pages that follow, I will give you the ingredients for pasta with and without eggs, and I will explain the three methods of making it at home.

Southern Italians make pasta either with or without eggs. If you've become addicted to homemade pasta but worry about cholesterol buildup, you can make eggless pasta with semolina, water, and a small amount of olive oil. I have provided two different sets of ingredients. The procedures are basically the same for semolina-water and egg-flour pasta, although the semolina is somewhat more difficult to work with and requires more kneading.

Homemade Pasta

Serves 4

Semolina-water pasta

2 cups semolina
2 tablespoons olive oil
⅔ to ¾ cup warm water
Pinch of salt

Egg-flour pasta

1½ to 2 cups unbleached flour
2 large eggs
Pinch of salt

By hand

1. Find a work surface where you have plenty of room. A wooden board on a kitchen counter will do, although it's easier to move around a free-standing table.
2. Pour the flour in a mound on one end of your work surface. If you dread messy cleanups, use a very wide, flat-bottomed wooden bowl.
3. In the center of the mound of flour make a hollow resembling a volcano crater. This is known as the well. If you are making semolina pasta, place the olive oil, ⅔ cup warm water, and the salt in the well. If you are making egg-flour pasta, put in the eggs and the salt. Stir with a fork to begin incorporating the flour from the inside wall of the well into the liquid. As the mixture thickens, set down your fork and begin mixing with your hands. You may have to add water to the semolina pasta or flour to the egg pasta to obtain a mixture that is soft but not sticky.
4. Work the pasta between the fingers of one hand and the heel of the other for 10 minutes or more if you are making semolina pasta, 8 to 10 minutes for egg pasta.
5. Set the dough down on a lightly floured work surface. Pull off a handful of dough, cover the rest with a towel to keep it from drying out, and roll out the pasta with a rolling pin. The rolled-out pasta sheet should be so thin you can read through it. Rotate the dough after each roll so that the sheet turns out more or less circular. To make it really thin, roll up about a third of the pasta from the far end of the sheet around your rolling pin. Roll the pin back and forth quickly, pressing the palms of your hands sideways into the dough so that it is stretched in two directions at once. Do this to all the dough, working quickly to prevent the pasta from drying out.
6. Drape a dish towel over the back of a chair or a pasta dryer and hang the pasta over it to dry for about fifteen minutes. It should look like fine leather.
7. To cut it into noodles, spread out the sheet, roll it up like a jelly roll, and slice the roll

¼ inch wide with a very sharp knife. Each slice will unroll into a noodle. If you are making macaroni, or some other tubular pasta, roll one-inch pieces of dough around a knitting needle or a chopstick, and press it to seal the cut ends together. Slip off each cylinder and let it dry on a towel.

In a food processor

1. With the steel knife in place, place the flour in the work bowl and turn the machine on and off.
2. Add the oil, water, and salt or the eggs and salt to the work bowl and process the mixture until it resembles cornmeal.
3. Gather the mixture together in your hands and press it to form a ball. Knead it by hand for 1 or 2 minutes until the dough is smooth and elastic. If you are continuing by hand, proceed with steps 4, 5, 6, and 7 of the directions for making pasta by hand (above). Otherwise go on to the next section.

In a hand-cranked pasta machine

1. Clamp the machine to the table or countertop, insert the handle and set the rollers at the widest opening.
2. Mix the pasta according to steps 2 and 3 in the directions for making pasta by hand (above). Knead the dough for a moment just to make it hold together. Then pass a handful through the rollers, covering the rest of the dough with a towel to prevent it from drying out. Repeat this procedure five or six times with the rollers set at the widest opening until the dough is smooth and elastic. Reset the dial to the next smaller opening and run the dough through. Continue until you have run through the number 5 or 6 opening. Repeat the procedure with the rest of the dough until you have smooth, translucent sheets. Dry them on dish towels hung over a pasta dryer or the back of a chair for 15 minutes.
3. Cut the pasta as in step 7 of the directions for making pasta by hand.

Cooking Pasta

1. Heat a four- or five-quart pot of water to a boil, add salt, and—when your sauce is almost ready—toss in the pasta. Freshly made pasta cooks in seconds after the water has returned to a boil. The pasta should not be overcooked but, as just about everybody knows by now, al dente, or just chewy. To check its progress, fish out a noodle, blow on it, and taste.
2. When the pasta is ready, turn it out into a colander or retrieve it with a spaghetti spoon or tongs and transfer it to the sauce. The sauce will cling better to the pasta if you toss the pasta with grated cheese first. If you drain the pasta in a colander, shake it a few times to make sure the water runs out the holes; otherwise you will water down your sauce. Another trick to making a perfect marriage between sauce and pasta is to add the pasta to the pan in which the sauce has been cooking and, over very low heat, toss them

together until every strand of pasta is coated with sauce. Whatever you do, don't bring the pasta to the table topped with sauce like an ice cream sundae. Those naked strands will turn cold rapidly. And do be sure to serve it immediately; if you let the pasta languish in the bowl, it will only be good for making Pasta Frittata.

Cleaning Squid

Your fish market might offer cleaned squid at premium prices, but you can do a better job in no time at home.

1. Take the tentacles in one hand, the sac in the other. Tug gently at the tentacles to detach them from the sac. Cut off the portion of the tentacles from the eyes down and discard. Reserve the tentacles.

2. Find the quill; it is a bone that looks as if it's made of plastic. Pull it out of the sac and discard it. Rinse the sac thoroughly under cold running water, peeling off the outer skin until the meat you have left is snow white. Hold the tentacles under running water and rub off as much of the outer skin as possible. Rinse the squid again and then pat it dry.

3. If you plan to use the squid ink, you must begin by removing the ink-filled sac across from the quill, being careful not to rupture it. This is most safely accomplished by holding the squid over a bowl that will catch the ink in case you do make a false move.

Peeling Tomatoes

Preparing fresh tomatoes for use in sauces is quick and easy.

1. Heat a pot of water (enough to cover a tomato) to boiling. Dip each tomato in the water until the skin loosens, about 1 minute.

2. Run the tomato immediately under cold water for a few seconds.

3. Use a fork and your fingers to lift off the skin.

Ingredients

Ingredients

Happily, the cuisines of the Mezzogiorno do not call for scores of hard-to-find ingredients. The one essential is freshness: unless the vegetables and cheeses you use in a dish are of truly fine quality, the end result will be disappointing. I'll never forget the morning I visited Palermo's historic outdoor market, the Vucciria, and a housewife at one stand took a look at the artichokes for sale—artichokes whose freshness would have been the envy of any American grocery shopper—and turned to the vendor with a sniff, telling him they were disgusting. You may wish to adopt a less confrontational approach, but you may be surprised at how eager to please your produce seller or fish vendor will be when he or she realizes you recognize the real thing.

Cheese

MOZZARELLA This cheese is Naples' trademark, and one reason that southern Italian cooking acquired a bad reputation in the United States is that so many restaurants have taken to melting an ersatz version over everything. That rubbery, plastic-wrapped product sold in supermarkets has no resemblance whatever to real mozzarella, and the casein product widely used as a pizza topping even less. True mozzarella is also known as *mozzarella di bufalo* because it is made from the milk of the water buffalo that wander the plains of Campania, and it is imported by air in minute quantities (which also makes it expensive). You can find a pure white, fresh version made from cow's milk (and known in Italy as *fior di latte,* or "flower of milk") in ethnic neighborhoods. Store it in the refrigerator for no more than a day or two in a container filled with water. Although some maintain it freezes successfully, I find it becomes watery.

PECORINO Used more frequently than genuine Parmigiano-Reggiano in southern Italy, this hard sheep's milk cheese is made in many parts of the Mezzogiorno and frequently grated over pasta. Sometimes it is studded with black peppercorns. In Sicily, pecorino is often enjoyed when still very young and soft and is known as *tuma* or, slightly older, as *primu sale*. In this book, since tuma is not available off the island, mozzarella is suggested as a substitute.

RICOTTA Whether made from whey or milk (whole or skim), ricotta is a creamy curd—technically not a cheese—that is used in countless dishes, from Neapolitan lasagne to the Sicilian sweet pastry, cannoli. Recommendations in many American cookbooks to the contrary, cottage cheese is absolutely not an acceptable substitute. Calorie counters need not despair, however; American part-skim ricotta is actually much closer in texture to the authentic Italian kind than is whole-milk ricotta.

RICOTTA SALATA "Salted ricotta" is easy to spot in Italian outdoor markets because it is shaped into a crown. Usually made from sheep's milk, it is grated over pasta in Sicily.

Vegetables

ARTICHOKES Unfortunately, it's difficult for Americans to obtain the young, tender artichokes that can be eaten whole as they are in Italy. The best you can do—short of raising them in your garden— is to choose only those with tightly closed leaves. For convenience, frozen artichoke hearts are a better bet than the marinated or canned ones.

BROCCOLI   Broccoli is especially popular as a simple sauce for pasta. In the market, look for heads without any yellow florets, with tender young buds that have not yet begun to open. You may notice the lovely purple-headed variety Italians often use; frankly, the purple tends to "wash out" in the cooking. Whichever color you use, just be sure not to overcook the vegetable or you will destroy the texture and flavor. Ten minutes for a whole head will usually do it.

BROCCOLI RABE   This vegetable looks something like a cross between broccoli and spinach. It has a slightly more bitter, more intense flavor than broccoli and is popular served on pasta.

CAULIFLOWER   When shopping, look for heads that are white, without any brown or yellow on the florets. Many people dislike cauliflower, usually because they have only eaten it cooked to a sour mush. Like broccoli, it should be cooked whole for no more than 20 minutes (less if it is a small head), or about 5 minutes for florets.

CHICORY   Also known as curly endive, this vegetable is used in soups and salads and is crisp and also slightly bitter.

EGGPLANT   In Sicily the eggplant—which arrived from India around 1600—is king. One restaurateur in Milazzo told me there were more than fifty ways to prepare it, and I'd call that a conservative estimate. In outdoor markets you find tiny eggplants (often sold in the U.S. as "baby eggplants"), which can be stuffed and served as individual portions. Although some consider it unnecessary, treating the eggplant by salting it and weighing it down with a heavy object (such as a cast-iron lid) overnight— or even just for an hour—gives excellent results in fried dishes. The liquid is drawn out and you can fry with a minimum of oil.

ESCAROLE   Coarse-leafed and slightly bitter, this green can be added to salads (use the inner leaves) and soups.

FLORENCE FENNEL   Also known as anise, this bulbous vegetable is a cousin of celery, and adds a wonderful flavor when the bulb is cut up and added raw to salads.

OLIVES   Although we often had olives at the table when I was growing up, I never liked them until I tasted them in Sicily. There, the majestic olive trees with silvery leaves seem, like the fig trees, to manage to grow everywhere. They produce fruit that is succulent, flavorful, and not at all bitter as are our chemically treated canned varieties, which should be avoided.

PEPPERS   For cooking, Italians use primarily bell peppers— green, or in their sweet red (mature) stage. The long yellowish type (sold as "Italian peppers") are good for frying. Dried red pepper—broken open and with seeds removed—is often added to sauces during cooking for piquancy.

TOMATOES   Americans may think southern Italian cuisine is entirely founded on the tomato, but natives take pride in the fact that many of their traditional recipes predate the fruit's arrival from the New World during the Spanish occupation. Nonetheless, tomatoes now have a place of honor, especially in Neapolitan kitchens; if you have visited Naples, you can appreciate how sweet, fresh tomatoes impart their glory to a dish in a way the canned kind can't. We don't always have access to fresh plum tomatoes, and if you do use the canned ones, they need sweetening to counteract their acidity (a task preferably accomplished with minced carrot, not sugar).

TOMATO PASTE   Making tomato paste in huge cauldrons is a time-honored tradition in southern Italy. There it's often sold commercially in tubes that can be squeezed out as needed, which is certainly handy. But while such tubes are imported on a limited basis, most of us have to make do with cans. To avoid ending up with a refrigerator full of moldy half-used cans, I spoon the paste into ice-cube trays and freeze it. One or two cubes can be added as needed to thicken and flavor a sauce.

SUN-DRIED TOMATOES   The first taste of a sun-dried tomato ranks among the memorable firsts of a lifetime; the concentration of tomato flavor is indescribably sweet. In Sicily and Calabria, fresh tomatoes in trays are placed outside in the sun, salted, and dried slowly. (Try it yourself if your yard is bathed in sunshine.) Jars of imported sun-dried tomatoes are sold in specialty food shops; don't be put off by the steep price, because a little goes a very long way in a salad or sauce.

ZUCCHINI   Every summer newspapers across the country print photographs of proud backyard gardeners wielding zucchini the size of baseball bats. Actually, the tastiest ones are small and narrow. The enormous, pale green variety sold in American ethnic markets as Sicilian Squash, on the other hand, typically weighs as much as five pounds. It is seeded, then boiled or braised.

Fish and Shellfish

CLAMS   Most shellfish from the Mediterranean and Adriatic seas is smaller and sweeter than that from colder North American waters. To approximate the Italian taste and tenderness, try littleneck clams. If you must buy canned ones, avoid the chopped variety; stick to the tiny, whole baby clams imported from the Orient.

SALT COD   Salt cod, or *baccalà,* is not only a Lenten and Christmas Eve favorite but popular year round. Because it is tough, it must be softened overnight and pounded before cooking.

MUSSELS   Fortunately, our mussels are delicious and inexpensive. In using them for such dishes as Linguine Fisherman's Style or Shellfish Risotto, be sure to scrape the shells with a scouring pad and a small knife, wash them well, and cut or pull off the beards (the black strings hanging from the shells).

SARDINES   Several of the classic Sicilian pasta and main courses feature fresh sardines, which can be difficult to obtain. If you insist on them, your fish seller will probably bring them from the market. Otherwise, try the quick-frozen imported kind (Portugal sends us good ones). Canned sardines won't do justice to traditional Sicilian dishes.

SHRIMP   Unless otherwise specified, use small fresh shrimp in the recipes in this book, removing the shells before cooking. To devein, cut the shell along the back and remove the black vein with a knife before shelling. Forget canned or frozen shrimp; they're lacking in taste and less convenient than fresh, anyway.

SQUID   Many Americans think that squid, or *calamari,* are repulsive because they look like octopus, which is a shame because they are delicious and tender as long as you don't overcook them. In particular, they make a wonderful sauce for pasta. For instructions on cleaning squid, see the instructions in the Techniques chapter (page 174).

TUNA   Fresh tuna, particularly popular in Sicily, has practically no resemblance in texture or flavor to the canned variety. The historic *tonnare,* or tuna hunts, of Trapani are now a popular tourist attraction.

Meats

PANCETTA   An unsmoked, Italian version of bacon, pancetta can never be replaced by American smoked bacon in recipes. If it isn't available, use boiled ham or prosciutto.

PROSCIUTTO   The best prosciutto, from northern Italy, is wonderfully delicate and not at all salty. What's available in most American markets doesn't quite measure up, and the government will not allow imports. Look for the Daniele brand (made in Rhode Island, with no preservatives) or Volpe.

SAUSAGE   Usually sold as "sweet" or "hot," Italian pork sausage sold here often contains fennel in addition to salt and pepper. Salami, a type of sausage, is dry and contains peppercorns and garlic; Genoa salami is the least fatty.

Nuts

ALMONDS   California almonds (unsalted, of course) work fine in southern Italian cooking. Sicilians, reflecting their Arab origins, add them to pasta, meat, fish, and dessert dishes.

PINE NUTS   These are the kernels of pine cones, sold in bulk in ethnic markets or in small (rather expensive) jars under the name "pignoli" or "pignolias." They add texture to a variety of sauces and fish dishes. If you can't find them, unsalted blanched almonds are an acceptable substitute.

PISTACHIOS   Sicilians use these in desserts, another Arab legacy. Be sure to use the natural type—pale to medium green—not the kind whose shells have been dyed red.

Rice

Long-grain rice is fine for use in casseroles, but for risotto try to find the short-grain Italian type labeled "Arborio" or "Ambra"; the rounded, pearly grains plump beautifully when cooked in broth.

Seasonings and Oils

BASIL   Even if you don't have a vegetable or herb garden, it's well worth growing a few small basil plants on your window sill; the sweetness of the fresh herb is an incomparable accompaniment to tomatoes. In some markets, fresh hydroponic (water-grown) basil is available year round.

BREAD CRUMBS   Sicilians like to sprinkle bread crumbs on pasta with fish sauces, and bread crumbs are used to add texture to many fish, meat, and vegetable dishes. Rather than buy the packaged kind, you can grate your own in a blender or food processor. If you do buy boxed bread crumbs, stay away from the kind with ''Italian seasonings''; these recipes call for dry unseasoned bread crumbs.

CAPERS   These are the buds of a wild plant that add texture and a slightly bitter flavor to sauces. Whether you buy the kind preserved in vinegar or salt, rinse them before using.

NUTMEG   Many people have never seen whole nutmegs, which can be used as needed—grated with a nutmeg grater or even the tines of a fork—for optimal flavor. Sicilians use it to flavor pasta and fish sauces.

FENNEL, WILD   In Sicily, except when the summer sun is blazing, wild fennel is there for the picking on the mountainsides. Unfortunately, it's all but unheard of here. Added to the pasta pot and to the traditional pasta con sarde it imparts a flavor that cannot be duplicated with Florence fennel (anise), but you might try using fresh dill, as Giuliano Bugialli suggests in *Classic Techniques of Italian Cooking*.

GARLIC   Would it surprise you to learn that I nearly forgot to include garlic on this list? Yes, it appears in many dishes in this book, fragrant but never overpowering. Those acrid, garlicky dishes served in American pizza parlors—the kind that leave you with pungent breath and queasy stomach—are seasoned with garlic powder, which ought to be outlawed.

PARSLEY   Use only fresh parsley, which can be stored in the refrigerator in a jar of water. The flat-leafed, Italian type is more flavorful than the curly.

VINEGAR   Although Italians have a number of specialty vinegars—most notably the strong balsamic type produced in the North—for ordinary cooking purposes, a good red wine vinegar is used in cooking.

OLIVE OIL   The imported extravirgin oils of northern regions, Tuscany and Liguria in particular, have awakened American palates to the taste of liquid gold. They are priced accordingly. Save them for uncooked or broiled dishes, such as salads and fish, when their flavor will truly shine through. For a change—and for fragrant, fruity olive taste at a lower price—try one of the south-

185

ern oils such as Madre Sicilia. (When you're in a calories-be-damned mood, by the way, you'll be amazed at how much flavor olive oil adds to deep-frying.) Avoid any olive oil that does not smell or taste of olives; who needs it?

SUNFLOWER OIL   For health reasons and for light deep-frying, try using sunflower oil. Rest assured, it's entirely authentic. Driving around Sicily you can't miss the fields of sunflowers growing beside the olive groves, vineyards, and fig orchards.

A Note On Wines

Southern Italian wines have come a long way in the past two decades. Although almost all of them used to be quite sweet and very high in alcohol content, today the area produces a number of wines of international repute. Although you still see the occasional hill covered with vines planted according to the *alborello* method—staked to form little trees that expose the grapes to too much hot southern sun—the trellised rows that produce drier wines are becoming more and more common.

After the arrival of the Greeks, the cult of Dionysius flourished in Sicily, and as early as the eighth century B.C. Hesiod wrote in detail about Beblino, a famous precursor of Moscato. In Roman times a temple consecrated to Venus stood high on the mountaintop at Erice, where the priestesses, who held prostitution sacred in the goddess's honor, apparently found time to drink a toast from time to time. The mountainside is still littered with amphorae that once contained Sicilian wines. Legend has it that the temple collapsed on the night Christ was born. Winemaking took a definite turn for the worse during the rule of the Arabs, who called a halt to viticulture and beheaded by scimitar anyone caught imbibing. Fortunately, however, after the Normans arrived, Arab-Sicilian poets began to sing the praises of the grape.

Marsala has long been the worldwide representative of Sicilian viticulture. Made of dry white wine blended with a mixture of brandy, sweet wine made from partly dried grapes (*passito*), and must, it is graded according to age. Many Americans keep a bottle handy to make zabaglione, the foamy egg and wine custard, but dry Marsala also makes an excellent aperitif. Marsala has been made in the western city of that name—originally Marsh-el-Alla, or Harbor of God—since the eighteenth century when British merchants, returning home with boatloads of wine, fortified it so that it would not turn to vinegar during the voyage; the British, already wild about port, quickly took its Sicilian cousin to heart. Rumor has it that one reason Garibaldi landed with such ease on the beach at Marsala in 1860 was that the Bourbons were reluctant to bombard the British wineries. In any case, Garibaldi and his Red Shirts are said to have refreshed themselves after coming ashore with a glass or two of Marsala at one of the city's wine shops.

Although Corvo red and white wines are widely credited with having brought Sicilian wines into modern times, they have been made since 1824. Corvo got its name from a rather gruesome local legend at Casteldacci near Palermo, where the Duca di Salaparuta founded his winery that year (the company of the same name is now run by Cinzano). An old man was bothered by a crow, the story goes. The villagers gave him a stick with which to kill it. After he did so, he gratefully stuck the stick into the ground and, lo and behold, it grew into a flourishing vine from whose grapes fine wines were made.

Other notable Sicilian wines are Alcamo, or Bianco d'Alcamo, a light, dry white; Etna red and white; Regaleali, a dry, straw-colored white produced in the interior; and the celebrated dessert wine Moscato di Pantelleria. Look for a *Q,* Sicily's mark of quality, on the label.

Campanian winemaking has an equally long history and no shortage of legends of its own. Taurasi, today considered one of the finest red wines in Italy, was known to the ancient Greeks, who introduced the Aglianico grape from which it is still made. In Roman times Pliny complained that some of the region's vines were getting out of hand and being allowed to sprout to treetop height, but he did offer praise for Falerno.

Lacrima Christi probably gets more attention because of its intriguing name (''tears of Christ'') than for its quality. One legend has it that the devil, when he fell from grace, fell to and hit the ground so hard that he hollowed out a great basin—the Bay of Naples. Realizing that he had landed on the closest place to Paradise, he populated the area with his devil disciples. When Christ saw what had happened, he wept, watering the slopes of Vesuvius to produce lush vines. According to another version of the tale, when Lucifer fell to earth, he managed to carry off a small piece of Paradise, which he dropped into the Bay of Naples—some say it was Capri—and the loss of something so lovely moved Christ to tears.

Campania also produces Greco di Tufo, a white D.O.C., (Denominazione d'origine Controllate) and the D.O.C. Ischia white and red. Basilicata's D.O.C. Aglianico del Vulture is considered one of southern Italy's best reds, and Calabria's red Cirò, produced in Catanzaro since ancient Greek days, is also noteworthy. Apulia produces a great deal of cutting wine and wines made into vermouth, as well as Sansevero, a D.O.C. white, red, and rosé.

Conversion Tables

The following are conversion tables and other information applicable to those converting the recipes in this book for use in other English-speaking countries. The cup and spoon measures given in this book are U.S. customary; use these tables when working with British Imperial or metric kitchen utensils.

Liquid Measures

The old Imperial pint is larger than the U.S. pint; therefore note the following when measuring the liquid ingredients.*

U.S.
Imperial
1 cup = 8 fluid ounces
½ cup = 4 fluid ounces
1 tablespoon = ¾ fluid ounce

1 cup = 10 fluid ounces
½ cup = 5 fluid ounces
1 tablespoon = 1 fluid ounce

U.S. Measure	Metric	Imperial*
1 quart	*946 ml*	*1½+ pints*
1 pint	*473 ml*	*¾+ pint*
1 cup	*236 ml*	*−½ pint*
1 tablespoon	*15 ml*	*−1 tablespoon*
1 teaspoon	*5 ml*	*−1 teaspoon*

Oven Temperatures

Gas Mark	¼	2	4	6	8
Fahrenheit	225	300	350	400	450
Celsius	107	150	178	205	233

*Note that exact quantities cannot always be given. Differences are more crucial when dealing with larger quantities. For teaspoon and tablespoon measures, simply use scant quantities, or for more accurate conversions rely upon metric measures.

Weight and Volume Measures

U.S. cooking procedures usually measure certain items by volume, although in the metric or Imperial systems they are measured by weight. Here are some approximate equivalents for basic items.*

	U.S. Customary	**Metric**	**Imperial**
Apples (peeled and sliced)	3 cups	500 g	1 pound
Beans, dried (raw)	2½ cups	450 g	1 pound
Butter	1 cup	250 g	8 ounces
	½ cup	125 g	4 ounces
	¼ cup	62 g	2 ounces
	1 tablespoon	15 g	½ ounce
Cheese (grated)	½ cup	60 g	2 ounces
Cornstarch	1 teaspoon	10 g	⅓ ounce
Cream of Tartar	1 teaspoon	3-4 g	⅛ ounce
Flour, all-purpose (sifted)	1 cup	128 g	4¼ ounces
	½ cup	60 g	2⅛ ounces
	¼ cup	32 g	1 ounce
Herbs, fresh	¼ cup whole	15 g	½ ounce
	2 tablespoons chopped	7 g	¼ ounce
Mushrooms, fresh (chopped)	4 cups	300 g	10 ounces
Nut meats	1 cup	112 g	4 ounces
Peas, fresh (shelled)	1 cup	450 g	1 pound
Potatoes (mashed)	2 cups	450 g	1 pound
Raisins (or Sultanas)	¾ cup	125 g	4 ounces
Rice	1 cup (raw)	225 g	8 ounces
	3 cups (cooked)	225 g	8 ounces
Spinach, fresh (cooked)	½ cup	285 g	10 ounces
Sugar: granulated	1 cup	240 g	8 ounces
	½ cup	120 g	4 ounces
	¼ cup	60 g	2 ounces
	1 tablespoon	15 g	½ ounce

*So as to avoid awkward measurements, some conversions are not exact.

	U.S. Customary	Metric	Imperial
confectioner's	*1 cup*	*140 g*	*5 ounces*
	½ cup	*70 g*	*3 ounces*
	¼ cup	*35 g*	*1+ ounce*
	1 tablespoon	*10 g*	*¼ ounce*
brown	*1 cup*	*160 g*	*5⅓ ounces*
	½ cup	*80 g*	*2⅔ ounces*
	¼ cup	*40 g*	*1⅓ ounces*
	1 tablespoon	*10 g*	*⅓ ounce*
Tomatoes, fresh (peeled, seeded, juiced)	*1½ cups*	*450 g*	*1 pound*
Zucchini	*3½ cups (sliced)*	*450 g*	*1 pound*
	2 cups (grated)	*450 g*	*1 pound*

Index